THE
SECRET
OF HOME

homesouls guide to abundant living

First published by O Books, 2008
O Books is an imprint of John Hunt Publishing
Ltd., The Bothy, Deershot Lodge, Park Lane,
Ropley, Hants, SO24 0BE, UK
office1@o-books.net
www.o-books.net

Distribution in:

UK and Europe
Orca Book Services
orders@orcabookservices.co.uk
Tel: 01202 665432 Fax: 01202 666219 Int. code
(44)

USA and Canada
NBN
custserv@nbnbooks.com
Tel: 1 800 462 6420 Fax: 1 800 338 4550

Australia and New Zealand
Brumby Books
sales@brumbybooks.com.au
Tel: 61 3 9761 5535 Fax: 61 3 9761 7095

Far East (offices in Singapore, Thailand, Hong
Kong, Taiwan)
Pansing Distribution Pte Ltd
kemal@pansing.com
Tel: 65 6319 9939 Fax: 65 6462 5761

South Africa
Alternative Books
altbook@peterhyde.co.za
Tel: 021 555 4027 Fax: 021 447 1430

Text copyright Lindsay Halton 2008

Design: Stuart Davies

ISBN: 978 1 84694 090 3

A CIP catalogue record for this book is available
from the British Library.

Printed in the US by Maple Vail

O Books operates a distinctive and ethical publishing philosophy in
all areas of its business, from its global network of authors to
production and worldwide distribution.
No trees were cut down to print this particular book. The paper is
100% recycled, with 50% of that being post-consumer. It's processed
chlorine-free, and has no fibre from ancient or endangered forests.
This production method on this print run saved approximately
thirteen trees, 4,000 gallons of water, 600 pounds of solid waste,
990 pounds of greenhouse gases and 8 million BTU of energy. On its
publication a tree was planted in a new forest that O Books is
sponsoring at The Village www.thefourgates.com

THE
SECRET
OF HOME

homesouls guide to abundant living

Lindsay Halton

BOOKS

Winchester, UK
Washington, USA

CONTENTS

CHAPTER 3   READING YOUR HOME

CHAPTER 4   homesouls® ORACLE READINGS

Your house is your larger body. It grows in the sun and sleeps in the stillness of the night; and it is not dreamless. Does not your house dream? And dreaming leave the city for the grove or the hilltop?

Kahlil Gibran, *The Prophet*

ACKNOWLEDGEMENTS

To the time it has taken to write this book, a period in which I have journeyed a long way and discovered a great deal: a time in my life when this was meant to be.

To the places through which I have gained so many insights, especially the Preseli hills in Wales where the rocks and the trees have spoken my language, and to my home, which has held so many messages. To my journey, which at times has been a real struggle, but which has given me the experience to write about what I know.

To all my family: most of all to Jackie for loving me and bearing with me, and for lending me her wisdom and experience. My children: Maelien, Charlotte and Louis, for helping me to work on what has been spoiled and for providing inspiration for drawings, not least for Charlotte's house, which has so much personality.

Amongst my family I include the voice that calls to me through the readings; I sometimes wish it had a face, but then perhaps its magic would be lost.

To Ed and Gill who supported us financially through much of the time it has taken to write this book, and for the love of Mum and Nan. To Dad for your inspirations: always ask why, and never wish to have your time over again.

To all my friends and clients, thanks for sharing your homes and stories with me and for being part of what I know.

Don't walk in front of me, I may not follow;
Don't walk behind me, I may not lead.
Just walk beside me and be my friend.

From me to you

I was a hero and a king in the inner world of my dreams, I was a lover, a warrior and a martyr as well, but in the outer world of appearances I could not see where I fitted in. I was seven years old and looking at my life through other people's eyes, sitting at my mother's side listening secretly to women's conversations, watching as teachers and adults moulded and shaped their children. Every night I returned to my dreams, to take off where I had left the night before, to experience another scene in what I sometimes believed to be my true story, for the wakeful world seemed too bizarre to be real. If it were real why would people hurt each other so much, why would they say the things they say and do the things they do? Why would teachers try to turn you into something you are not? Why couldn't every parent recognise how unique their children were, and why were children so cruel? This was not the way it seemed to everyone but it was the first scene in my life story. It set the stage for what was to come.

Eighteen years of education and seven years working as an architect, I played Sonny Boy Williamson: "I ain't fattening no more frogs for snakes", and I heard my mentor's voice: "Find your place of value in this world full of facts".

In 1992 I looked at my children and moved to another scene in our lives, something was calling us West to a wild place where we might find sanctuary from the rub of modern life. I left my job and the security of city life; together we left the smog and found the mist where the invisible and the manifest meet to call through the annals of time.

To the East of our home is Caerfyrddin, "Merlin's town", and to the West is Carn Ingli, "the Hill of Angels". Little did I know that I was moving to a place so steeped in mystery and magic and to a time that would reveal so many illusions.

I took a leap of faith and began a journey with the I Ching, to a magical landscape hidden in the details of my place and time. The dragons came out of my shadows with inspiration and guidance and I discovered just how much of life is staged and scripted, and just how much we choreograph the physical conditions of our bodies. We breathe life into our stories and they take shape in the places that surround us.

I journeyed deeper through my inner landscape, and discovered how to become a better architect, not designing homes but helping others to see their homes as a mirror of themselves. I learned to guide people deeper into their stories and to see the home as a vehicle to a more fulfilling life.

In the Wild West of Wales in the landscape I call my home, the veil between this world and beyond is thin. In many unsigned places I can still feel the pulse of the hidden landscape, its pulse beats to the rhythm of my Soul, I can feel it beating in my heart. Here it is easier for me to tune in.

In so many other places the veil has become thick, like smog building layer upon layer, a heavy garment through which it is difficult to see clearly. We stretch the smog across every aspect of our humanity, woven by our own minds, thread by thread one illusion at a time. We clip each other's wings and we clip our own, yet at the same time we long to soar so high and to see clearly the experience of our own lives.

A mother grows tired of nurturing others and forsaking herself – yet she persists. A father scolds a child unjustly – bestowing one more piece of emotional baggage to carry. The lover hurts by being unfaithful, the boss by being so controlling, and all of us by not being what someone else wants us to be.

Thread by thread we weave the smoggy web through which we cannot see and in which we cannot breathe the breath of freedom we all cherish so much. We all feel such loss many times throughout our lives, and we long for a brighter and clearer horizon. Our longing calls us home – it is our guide.

The Welsh have a word for this longing; they call it "Hiraeth" (pronounced "hear-eye-th") the most Soul-filled word in the Welsh language: warm like heart and hearth, but with no literal trans-lation into English. Occasionally I ask Welsh audiences what this word means to them. They pause for thought, and usually say it means longing or homesickness. They give the dictionary definition, but always gesture with a glint in the eye and the hand reaching out from the heart, as if the word emanates from the heart – the gesture says it all. Our heartstrings connect us with what we long for.

→   Dora Polk, in her book _Hiraeth_ says: _"Hiraeth… looks back as well as forwards, to a state that the Soul enjoyed before it entered the vale of tears and will resume again after the body expires"._

In this vale of tears we journey through our lives. Here in this vale there is work to be done, space to be nourished and wounds to be healed. It takes courage to walk here, and especially to pause and wonder why we are here, and how we can best be of service.

At the gates of Heaven we might well consider how well we have lived. How well did we walk through that valley, and what have we learned, as we reflect on the tears shed while we watered our path with so much joy and so much pain in weaving the story that was once our life. It all comes to pass in the blink of an eye, for the space we inhabit is without boundary and without time, it is here and now, forever and always.

Through getting to know my home more deeply, I have come to see myself and my place in the world more clearly. The journey with my home has been a healing experience, full of revelations, sometimes hard and sometimes fun, but always rewarding. The Secret of Home and the Glass Runes were born from my journey. I feel gifted and blessed by their inspiration and commission to cast them into the world. Thirteen years ago I heard a voice upon the wind, it said:

Clever things and clever places
Conceal the wounds on many faces.

Remove the mask that hides the wound
And reveal the shroud of an empty room.

Hollow rooms devoid of grace
Cut deeply into nature's face.

In Meditation, Lindsay Halton, 1994

This was my calling to do this work. Each page of this book has been a step on my journey, usually a flash of inspiration followed by a long period of waiting and watching as the truth behind the inspiration showed itself in the circumstances of my life. On a wish and a prayer I cast the Secret of Home and the Glass Runes into the world.

What can this book do for you?

The way to Be
In the hidden landscape of oneself
On the journey of one's life
To find the way home

The Secret of Home will help you step back and take a wider view of the way things are affecting your life, placing the small things that happen to you within the bigger picture of your life as a whole, to help you see beyond your immediate situation. The readings of the homesouls Oracle will help you to make choices by placing your current issues within the context of your life as a whole. The Glass Runes offer inspiration and have spiritual authority and offer practical guidance to point the way forward in our lives. They walk us through an imaginative house opening doors to hidden rooms where we lock away our deeper thoughts and emotions. The homesouls Oracle readings are words of inspiration to greet you at the threshold: invitations for you to enter and go deeper with the journey of your life, to know the way of changes that will best serve the Calling of your life.

We are all self builders: alchemists engaged in a process of reconstruction, working with the elements of our lives to recreate ourselves, building invisible walls with room to hold our dreams and hide away our shadows, constructing facades as a way to present ourselves to the world. The physical world is but a reflection of the invisible world. The houses we live in mirror much deeper aspects of ourselves that inhabit our hearts and minds. The Secret of Home will help you find yourself within the mirror of your home. It will guide you to enter the looking glass, seeking a truer reflection of the way things are meant to be.

The way you see the world is the way it is.
Change your view, then your experience will change too.

The elements have so much to tell us. Beyond the mirror there is so much to be seen, and the more I look, the more I find. The more I find, the more I have to write about. It would give me great pleasure to immerse myself in the world beyond the looking glass, and so I am wary to keep my feet firmly on the ground, this side of the window. Building and farming, I get my hands dirty, and this keeps me here and now. So I must warn you, right at the beginning, this journey into your home may take you somewhere you have not been before.

I present the subject lightly, but don't let this catch you out, the Secret of Home may take you deeply into your story and things that need healing may come to the surface. My role is not to be just an author (as much as I would like that), I have to be a responsible guide, and an architect, building something that will serve us, and that will last. Some people will need support to find their way around this wheel, some will need help to interpret a plan or an image, others will need emotional support, and two heads are often better than one. So in advance of the book launch I have developed a website, a home for homesouls, which I hope will become an online meeting place for readers and consultants to share their thoughts, findings, and concerns. www.homesouls.com and www.glassrunes.com

I have visited hundreds of homes, in my capacity as a homesouls consultant, looking at how intimately the life of each person is connected with the details of their home.

This book is my way of sharing my experience and under-standing, in the hope that others will be inspired to look more deeply as I have. If this idea captures your imagination, I am sure, like me, that you will be drawn into it. And I hope like me, you will find the Secret of Home with the homesouls Oracle readings a good guide for your journey.

You are now standing at the threshold, perhaps questioning:

Curious – What is in this book for me?
Doubtful – Is this journey for me?
Excited – Can I dive straight in?

If any of these questions are in your mind, then perhaps you need a little taster, a first bite of the cherry, a brief encounter, to give you some idea of what the Secret of Home can offer you.

The Journey starts with a question. You could ask:

What is in it for me?
or
What issue in my life should I work upon now?

If you want to make this little excursion, go to the contents page and turn to:

• Rooms and Runes – The Way into your Story
• How to use the Glass Runes

After that little excursion, to make sense of it all, I suggest you come back to continue the journey from here; beginning with the notion that your life story is reflected in the details of your home.

Your home is a mirror of your life.

Chapter 1

Living in your story

A life coaching tool

I started on this book in 1996, or perhaps I should say it started on me. At that time Feng Shui was enjoying the limelight, having journeyed for thousands of years, and thousands of miles, across the divide between East and West, it came to us like a fast moving train.

If I wanted to be up front I had to jump on quickly – a major publisher was pushing me for the script. I was tempted, I must admit, but decided to hold back because something was growing in me that was not quite Feng Shui, and I was not ready to birth ideas and experiences that had not quite settled in me. The gestation period was eleven years, through to this time in 2007. The ideas have travelled a long way with me, through a lot of experience, and a lot of houses.

Responding to the voice I heard upon the wind in 1994, I took my call: *"hollow rooms devoid of grace cut deeply into natures face"*, and I jumped into the deep end with my work.

Homesouls was called Hiraeth Feng Shui then, based on an idea that there is a heartfelt calling of the Soul, and we can dialogue with this calling by working with our homes.

I was working with my hunches, following leads where they took me. I seemed to be able to tap into people's lives, to find a strong correlation between how they were in their lives, and how they were in their homes.

I discovered how to see the bigger picture, as if I had a looking glass through which I could see their lives reflected in the details of their homes.

My wife Jackie was a Shiatsu therapist, and she had taught me the language of the Five Elements (an oriental concept), underlying the conditions that affect change in our lives.

My mind was awash with these experiences, and with the

possibilities of where I could go with them. I was an architect, and I was stepping over the line, taking a risk that British architects are not supposed to take. I was stepping away from pragmatic considerations, into a world that was surreal, or perhaps super-real.

In a way this was an escape from one side of the track where life was too much like a prison, with too many people saying, "how can I make a difference, my hands are tied" – those suits, like straight jackets, too constricting to hold me any more. On the other side of the track, things did not look much better. The New Age seemed so needy. Nobody there said my hands are tied, but so many were greedy, reaching out, desperate for information, and for stuff to heal the body and the home, on a quest for enlightenment that seemed to have become a shopping bazaar.

I did not want to catch that train, and so I was stuck in the middle, looking for another way. The middle way for me was not right down the centre, but to walk my talk as if the tracks were not really there. Then it occurred to me that I was already doing just that. Most days I walked with my dog, called Beauty, through a clearing along an old railway line, along the riverbank leading to a Stone Age burial chamber. This was our route, a slow walk, and a dip in the river for the dog; no train, no clatter, and no clutter, just being in the moment. This was the way I had decided to approach my work, and this is the way my book has found its form.

In January 1996 I visited a spiritual medium, highly recommended by friends that I trusted. It had to be that way, because when it came to mediums and psychics, I was more than a little cautious and sceptical. I still am. This man, Laurence Harry, told me things that even I did not know. He told me that my grandfather was gassed during the war, and that my mother left home when she was very young, he even journeyed in his mind to the exact house where she lived, naming the street.

I questioned my mother afterwards, and she confirmed that my grandfather was gassed, which is the reason why the gas supply was removed at his request from our house, and yes, she had lived where Laurence had said.

I kept my cards close to my chest, I did not tell him anything, not even that I was writing this book. It was then called *A Blueprint for Living*, taking inspiration from the way that architects used to copy their drawings onto blueprints, and the idea that the ancient Feng Shui plan, the Bagua, is a blueprint that holds the stories of our lives. Laurence said he was communicating with my ancestors, guardians and guides, and he relayed a message that I should be working on "a blueprint for life". That was just what I needed to hear at that time, I needed that affirmation to have more faith in my path and to work wholeheartedly with my calling. Two and a half years later I was able to repay my gratitude to Laurence, when he asked me to do a reading for him and his wife Jayne.

Sometimes we all reach a point in life where we feel muddled, with too many or unclear options, we don't know what to do or which way to turn. This book will help you navigate through these difficult times, offering practical guidance to help you find what you are looking for.

Healing the body and easing emotional pain may seem so hard at times, but in the home there is always something that you can do to affect the way things are in your life. Opportunities are always close at hand and truth is always waiting to be discovered. With what I term *homesouls*, interior design becomes an everyday prayer and the Glass Runes become a way into the story of your life and your home.

I feel blessed to have entered so many lives and so many homes over the past twelve years, and thank all my clients for having paved the way for this homesouls Oracle, which I have called the Secret of Home.

The phone rings and someone asks me to visit their home to give them advice. Immediately I make it clear that I do not want to know anything about their home or their life because it is important for me to prepare myself in an intuitive way without making any judgements. So we agree the date and the fee for the consultation, and when the time comes I make my intuitive preparations, knowing only their name and address and nothing else about their life and home. I give myself some time and find some space to feel that I am focused on what I am about to do. I write their name and address down and turn to the Oracle for advice.

That was how I approached the reading for Laurence and Jayne, except in those days I used the I Ching. Nowadays I have my own homesouls Oracle, and the Glass Runes to guide me. I ask the Oracle questions about my clients and about their home, and guided by this script my intuition seems to open to the flow of information. Some people call this channelling, streaming or downloading. I just think of it as intuition. Often specific and very personal information comes flooding to me. I write down my thoughts as if writing in a conscious stream from a flow that is connected to their life story. This is a crucial part of my work because I gain insights that may not have come to me in any other way. The information is a gift to me and I know I can trust the process because I have done it successfully so many times.

So with Laurence and Jayne, as with all of my clients, we began with an in-depth personal chat and then I revealed what I had already written down. I also showed them an image I had sketched before I came to them.

This is the sketch and an extract from what I wrote:

'Thunder has penetrated the rain clouds, so tension is released. The thunderstorm breaks and the whole of nature breathes freely. Now you have been carried to the top of the Mountain, you must take time in this place; the force of the wave that has swept you forward has left things undone. You must pause now, take time for contemplation. Review the past, release the tension that is still in the air, forgiving misdeeds and transgressions- let them go – sweep them away – clear the air in preparation to move on. Be clear about your intentions before you move. Hasty decisions built upon insecure foundations lead to failure. Be still, don't try to move too quickly.'

This made a lot of sense to them, in some ways it made more sense to them than it made to me, after all the image was intended for them. The image and the reading reflected so many of their issues. Unknown to me, they were at that time seriously considering moving from Wales to Canada, but their planning was fraught with problems. They saw in the image so many unresolved issues that they could not leave behind. Laurence said he was still angry about things in the past, he wanted to release the anger and the tension. In the context of their story, THUNDER was a call for forgiveness, to release the anger and tension that was bottled up. WATER was a call for taking their time, and MOUNTAIN called for being still, taking good care of themselves, and creating firm foundations to build the rest of their lives upon. These elements of Thunder, Water, Mountain, appear in my drawing.

There are five more elements, each has its own story to tell, and each has its own place within the house, and unity is the point in the middle, where everything is connected.

There is always an image that fits the issue. The body presents us with a picture of health, that reflects the way things are in our lives, and so does the house. Usually I will find these images when I go to a client's house, and the purpose of this book is to help you find the image in your home, and to work with the issues held within the images you find. The details of your home are symptoms of what is going on in your life. For Laurence and Jayne, I took the image with me, but usually the image is already present within the home, perhaps in the leaking pipes, or problems with the doors, or perhaps more clearly focused in a picture on the wall or the contents of a cabinet. More about this later.

Laurence said of the image: *"The doorway is a mirror, all I need to do is work through that illusion"*. Jayne saw the doorway as a mirror that seemed restricting, not a true picture of her, but a thinner version, as if she were a teenager. The mound, she said, was a pregnant tummy, *"I feel uncomfortable with the mound showing, and I want to bring the water up"*. Jayne's issues were in the EARTH element, these relate to pregnancy, motherhood, and being stuck, and her body was presenting problems in her womb at that time. We looked at the areas of THUNDER, WATER and EARTH in their home, and we discussed what could be done to make those areas present a better picture of what they wanted to see in their lives.

My clients are often stunned by the accuracy of the information and by the personal details that are contained in my house reading. They feel they can trust me because they know I have not judged them, but have received their story in a spirit of openness and acceptance. Generally, because I have read their situation correctly, they will accept my guidance about where to look in their home and how to work with what they find.

When I leave my clients, they feel inspired and enthusiastic, they can see their homes as a reflection of their lives and they feel motivated to make some changes. Often they report that the advice I have given in one day has kept them going for two years or more, but when this time is over I want them to have the tools and the information to keep the process going. So the Secret of Home has been scripted as a tool for self-help, to aid the journey of one's life, having evolved from the inspirations I received through my client consultations.

The Secret of Home with the Glass Runes are a life coaching tool. They will not give you definitive answers nor will they solve any problems for you, but they will help you to gain insights into the bigger picture of what is going on in your life, and will guide you to look in the right place.

We need a map to start our journey.

Thousands of years ago, a Chinese sage found our map on the shell of a turtle. This mystical creature had an arrangement of markings on its back, which the sage took to be numerically related to the order of the universe. Chinese philosophers then began to write about these markings as the <u>eight elemental forces that shape our lives</u>. They gave these forces a context through which they could understand the workings of the universe. It has now become known as <u>the *Bagua*</u> – this is our map. I call it <u>the Invisible Plan</u>. It is <u>the image behind</u> one of the oldest books of wisdom in the world <u>the I Ching</u>.

The Invisible Plan is a blueprint for life, <u>a life map</u> that sets the scene through which we now enter the homesouls story.

I am not a scholar of Chinese philosophy, but an architect and an explorer. I have used their map to explore the invisible landscape, and have seen its reflections in many homes and many lives, so I know the territory and I can take you there. Let me guide you to wander and wonder through the inner landscape of your life and home.

This is a mythical journey so don't take it literally, it is just a story, but you will be amazed how true it all is.

The author C.S. Lewis once said: *"There is only one creator and we* merely mix the elements he gives us," and to this, in her book *What the Bee Knows* P.L. Travers added: *"Elements among elements, we are there to shape, order, define, and in doing this we, reciprocally, are defined and shaped and ordered. The potter, moulding the receptive clay, is himself being moulded."*

The I Ching presents us with ancient wisdom along this story line, uncovering a blueprint for life based upon the eight elements of change. Richard Wilhelm's translation sums this up: *"Underlying reality there is a world of archetypes, and reproductions of these make up the real things in the material world."*

The eight elements are undercurrents to everything that happens, each element reflecting what goes on in the different areas of our lives.

We come to know them as concepts or ideas. In essence they have no real form and come from a formless space that we perceive through the imagination. Their presence can be seen all around us: in the forces of nature, in personalities and characteristics, in physical appearances and in the design and aesthetics of the home.

These archetypal energies are the moving forces of our lives, they are catalysts for change, and how we respond to them affects the qualities of life we experience.

the potter, molding the receptive clay, is herself being molded.

The map is the plan of your house.

To start the journey you will need the map, so draw a basic plan of your home, it does not need to be accurate, but try to get it roughly in proportion. Read on a few pages before you start your drawing in your journal.

Here are two examples:

House One

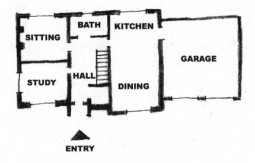

House Two

Start a home journal

Getting to know your home more deeply will help you to see your life more clearly.

It helps at this stage to begin a home journal to log the way things are right now, what you do in your home, and how things change. It will be useful as a kind of travel log, to look back over the steps you have taken, and to track your story as it unfolds.

I suggest you organise your home journal into nine chapters, to correspond with the nine scenes of the plan. Perhaps you can start your journal by drawing a plan of your house on the first page.

When you combine the house plan you have drawn with one of the plans on the next page – the Magic Square or the Wheel of Changes, you will have a life map that sets the scene to view your home as a mirror of your life.

Locate the Invisible Plan within your home

The interior of your home reflects the things that matter in your life. Its nine areas form the Invisible Plan that in Feng Shui is called the Bagua. This plan is like a painter's palette and its elements are the ingredients we work with in the story of our lives.

The basic plan in the form of the Magic Square, or Wheel of Changes is the blueprint for our life stories. Your home will be a variation of this blueprint.

Consider the whole plan of your home as if it were imprinted in the landscape. It is this footprint that defines the place of your story. The story of your life has its scenes, not written into the chapters of a book but embodied within the plan of your home. The plan is like a stage with nine areas and each area holds a scene from your life story.

There are two ways to draw the Invisible Plan:

The Magic Square   The Wheel of Changes

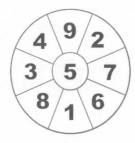

4	9	2
3	5	7
8	1	6

Scene 1.	WATER	Blue Rune
Scene 2.	EARTH	Yellow Rune
Scene 3.	THUNDER	Green Rune
Scene 4.	WIND	Orange Rune
Scene 5.	UNITY	Clear Rune
Scene 6.	HEAVEN	White Rune
Scene 7.	LAKE	Turquoise Rune
Scene 8.	MOUNTAIN	Purple Rune
Scene 9.	FIRE	Red Rune

How to orientate the plan to your home

- Draw your house plan with the main entrance door at the bottom of the page.
- The main entrance is not always the front door or the most impressive entrance.
- The main entrance can be considered as the mouth of your home, through which you, your family, friends, and nourishment enter most frequently.
- If more than one door is used in this way, then you must decide which door seems like the mouth of your home.
- When you draw the Invisible Plan, numbers 8, 1, 6 are at the bottom of the page.
- Overlay the Invisible Plan onto the plan of your house and you will see that you first pass through either 8 (Mountain), or 1 (Water), or 6 (Heaven) as you enter your house.

How do the numbers map out in your house?

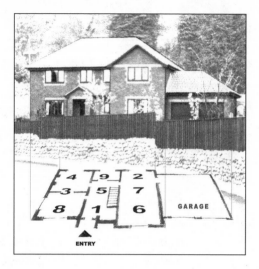

In a square or rectangular house plan, the nine areas are easy to locate.

4	9	2
3	5	7
8	1	6

4	9	2
3	5	7
8	1	6

- If your house is not a square or rectangle shape, then you need to consider which parts of the plan are projected, and which parts are missing.
- Whatever your house shape, start by drawing either of the above regular shape plans divided into nine squares as shown. The plan has four external walls and each wall is divided into thirds.

- **A projection** may be slightly wider than one third of the wall; it will never be wider than two thirds of the wall.

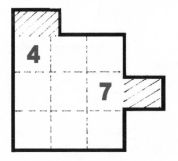

In this plan areas 4 and 7 have projections.

- **A missing area** may take up slightly more than one square, but it will never take up two full squares.

In this plan areas 8 and 7 are missing

- Some houses have both projections and missing areas.

In this plan areas 9 and 6 have projections and areas 8 and 7 are missing

The Invisible Plan with its nine areas fills the interior of your home. In some really odd-shaped houses it makes more sense to divide the plan using the Wheel of Changes rather than the Magic Square.

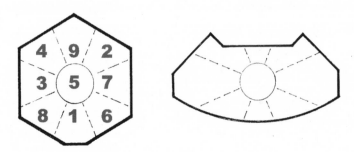

Don't be too rigid about establishing the boundaries of each area. The nine areas are quite fluid, perhaps a better diagram could be made with watercolour on wet paper, as then the margins between each area would be more loosely defined.

This is why you can use either the Magic Square or Wheel of Changes plan because they both offer a rough guide that will take you close enough to the same areas of your home.

Once you have grasped the idea of how the invisible plan exists within your house plan, I want you to loosen the concept, allowing the shape of your home to define the shape of the invisible plan.

The Invisible Plan seems too rigid when the Magic square or the Wheel of Changes is drawn onto a house plan. The lines are only guides, so it is better to define the position of the elements within your home according to what is there.

For instance, you can see in the plan below that in my old farmhouse with its new extension the area of WIND is missing, and WIND is relatively small in comparison to THUNDER. I have included the boundary walls and the windows as part of the WIND area. LAKE is both sides of a separating wall, and WATER has an odd shaped boundary. My house, like most houses does not divide neatly into nine squares so I have had to decide how the Invisible Plan exists within my house plan.

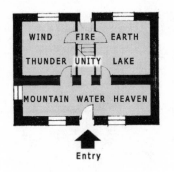

In my old farmhouse, the main entrance shown here was actually the back door, as this was the door we used most often.

My old farmhouse

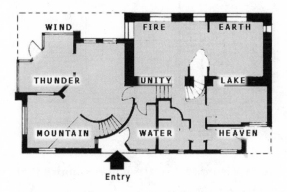

My old farmhouse with new extension

After rebuilding and extending my old farmhouse, the plan now has a more irregular shape. Compare this with the original old farmhouse plan above to see how the invisible plan has stretched to fill the new place.

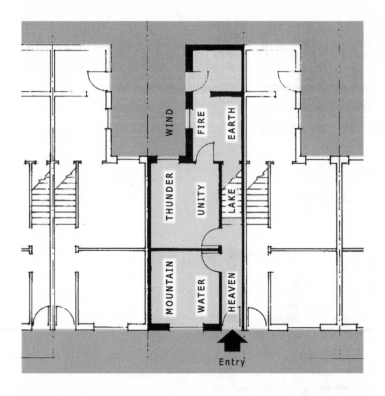

Above is a typical British Victorian Terrace house – notice that the square number 4 (WIND) is missing.

If your place is an apartment or a one-room bed-sit in a shared house, then place the invisible plan in your personal space. Other people's places have their own invisible plans.

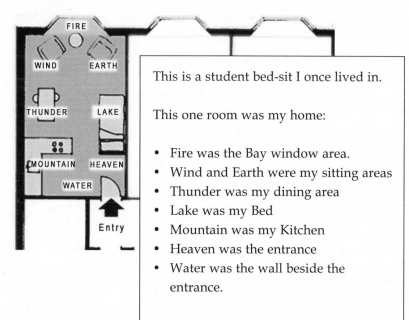

This is a student bed-sit I once lived in.

This one room was my home:

- Fire was the Bay window area.
- Wind and Earth were my sitting areas
- Thunder was my dining area
- Lake was my Bed
- Mountain was my Kitchen
- Heaven was the entrance
- Water was the wall beside the entrance.

The other tenants' rooms had their own invisible plans

The garage and the annexe

Unless the garage or the annexe is an integral part of the house, don't include it in the plan.

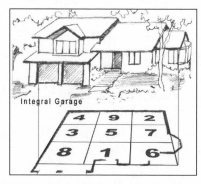

This garage is integral, forming part of the invisible plan because it has bedrooms over it.

This garage is attached but not part of the main house and so it does not form part of the invisible plan.

A lot of people enter their homes through the garage, but the garage door is not the mouth of the house, neither is the internal door between the garage and the house.

If in doubt, pretend that I am to call at your house – the door you would tell me to call at is the mouth of your house.

Missing areas

My old farmhouse with its new extension has missing areas. You can see that WIND and part of HEAVEN are missing. If your home has missing areas, they may not hold the main issues in your life right now, but at some stage they will call for your attention. Missing areas are not bad, they simply reflect the way life is; that some parts of our lives need more attention than other parts.

The boundaries of the plan

With homesouls we consider the bigger picture in the whole story of our lives and so we focus on the main floor of our homes where our public and private lives meet. This is generally the floor that contains the Kitchen/Dining, Living and Reception rooms. As a student I occupied just one room and so my Invisible Plan just filled that space. In a single storey house the bedrooms would be included in the Invisible Plan because they occupy the main floor with the Kitchen/Dining and Living rooms. In a house with more than one storey you need only work on your issues at the main floor level. If you want to look at the upper or lower floors then consider the plan rising through these floors as well.

Questions about the plan:

Question: Can I place the Invisible Plan within each individual room?

Answer: No – Just overlay the Invisible Plan over your whole house plan.

Some people might be inclined to place the Invisible Plan on each individual room, because this is what is done in Feng Shui. Then you would have an additional nine areas to consider within each room, and in my experience this is too much – you need only consider the bigger picture. Consider the whole house plan, for this holds the blueprint of your whole life story. In the bigger picture individual rooms occupy a particular scene within the Invisible Plan and are deeply connected with that particular area of your life story.

Don't be tempted to work in too many areas of your home at once. Focus your attention on one particular issue at a time and don't work on more than two areas at a time. If you try to do too much at once you will lose your focus and scatter your energy.

Question: What if I occupy just one part of a house, or an apartment within a bigger building?
Answer: Apply the Invisible Plan to your own habitable space. Other people living in other places will have their own Invisible Plans.

If you occupy just one part of a house, as I did in my student days, then your Invisible Plan will occupy this one area. In this situation, each individual in the house has their own individual plan occupying their personal space. In family homes and shared houses we all occupy the same space and so the whole house plan is what we need to look at.

Question: Is it okay for me to work on my own issues, when someone else shares the space with me?
Answer: Absolutely yes.

When we live together our issues are closely connected. The analogy of the butterfly taking flight in the rainforest is suitable here: its motion affects the wind and eventually the change in wind is felt in other parts of the world.

As you work on your issues in the home, the winds of change ripple through the lives of all those you are connected to. The choices you make affect the lives of everyone, but you need not fear the effect you will have, because as long as your intentions are true and just and you act authentically, then you can welcome the changes you bring. Often companions will be happy for you to make the changes you want within your home, but if they want more input then the dialogue that goes on between you is an important part of the transformation process.

Rooms and Runes – The way into your story

The Glass Runes

The Wheel of Changes directs you to eight places around the plan of your home, and one in the middle. It is also a compass pointing to the location of each Glass Rune on the wheel. The Glass Runes are an ideal tool for working with the homesouls Oracle, but they are not essential. If you have not purchased the Glass Runes with this book, you can buy them online at **www.glassrunes.com**.

If you want to use a substitute, the simplest method is to use rolled up paper, doing readings is then a bit like choosing a ticket in a raffle. Use nine small pieces of paper of equal size, write on each one the colour of the Rune it represents and the element it relates to.

ORANGE **WIND** 4	RED **FIRE** 9	YELLOW **EARTH** 2
GREEN **THUNDER** 3	CLEAR **UNITY** 5	TURQUOISE **LAKE** 7
PURPLE **MOUNTAIN** 8	BLUE **WATER** 1	WHITE **HEAVEN** 6

Throughout the book I will be referring to the Glass Runes, I intend this to mean the rolled up paper version as well, but for simplicity I will always refer to the Glass Runes.

GLASS RUNE	ELEMENT	QUALITY	HIGHEST POTENTIAL
CLEAR RUNE	UNITY	TAI CHI	Everything is connected
BLUE RUNE	WATER	FLOW	Faith in your journey
PURPLE RUNE	MOUNTAIN	STABILITY	The strength to be who you truly are
GREEN RUNE	THUNDER	AUTHORITY	Forgiving and giving your blessing
ORANGE RUNE	WIND	DRIVE	Following a personal code of honour
RED RUNE	FIRE	TRUTH	Managing power with truth and love
YELLOW RUNE	EARTH	RELATING	Choosing companions wisely
TURQUOISE RUNE	LAKE	INNOCENCE	Truly loving yourself
WHITE RUNE	HEAVEN	BOUNDARIES	Making choices that reflect your highest purpose

Clear Rune of UNITY, meaning all is one. It calls for us to find our way home, to know contentment; then all is well and there is nothing to be done.

Blue Rune of WATER is flowing. It calls for courage, faith and trust on the journey of our lives.

Purple Rune of MOUNTAIN is all knowing. It calls for us to know ourselves and to find tranquillity and contentment through being in this world.

Green Rune of THUNDER is empowering. It calls for us to know our own authority, and to use our power wisely, knowing the value of blessing and forgiveness.

Orange Rune of WIND is abundant. It calls for us to act honourably through processing the changes in our lives.

Red Rune of FIRE is radiant. It calls for us to shine, and to follow our true paths.

Yellow Rune of EARTH is nourishing. It calls for us to nourish the people, places and things in our lives, and to choose our companions wisely.

Turquoise Rune of LAKE is loving. It calls for us to see the hidden beauty of all things, to know the joy of innocence and to be creative.

White Rune of HEAVEN knows life's calling. It calls us to make choices that serve our higher purpose.

How to use The Glass Runes

Consider an issue you have in your life and ask the Oracle for guidance. It can be anything. You might have a relationship or career issue, a cash flow problem or self-esteem issue.

To do a reading you hold a question or a request in mind, for example:

"I would like some guidance on this issue".
or
What issue should I work on now?

You don't need to say it aloud you can simply think it.

1. With your question or request in mind give the bag of Glass Runes a shake.
2. Without looking, take one Glass Rune from the bag (note the colour).
3. Return the Rune to the bag and shake the bag again.
4. Without looking, take a second Rune.
5. These two Runes in the order you chose them will give you a reading.
6. Refer to the Readings index in Chapter 4.

Note: If you are using rolled up paper instead of Glass Runes you could choose them from a small box or a hat, in the same way that you would choose winning raffle tickets.

Every issue has a place somewhere in your home. So to work on an issue you need to know:

Where in my home does this issue live?
or
Where in my home should I work on this issue?

• With your question in mind take just one Rune from the bag.

- This Rune represents the place where your issue lives within your life and home.
- Turn to Chapter 2 – Through the Looking Glass, and read the scene that relates to the Glass Rune that you have chosen.
- If you do not yet know how to locate the area in your home, then go back several pages to read how to locate the area in the plan.

WELSH RUNE

In this fateful hour,
I call upon all heaven with its power
And the sun with its brightness
And the snow with its whiteness
And the fire with all the strength it hath
And the lightning with its rapid wrath
And the winds with their swiftness along the path
And the sea with its deepness
And the rocks with their steepness
And the earth with its starkness
All these I place,
By Heaven's almighty help and grace,
Between myself and the powers of darkness.

Traditional verse

When I started to do readings in 1995, I would prepare myself before meeting the client at their home. I had three methods of gathering information. First I would ask the I Ching for guidance, then I would use the Viking Runes for further clarification, and then I would look at the birth chart of the client using 9 Star KI astrology.

With each new consultation I relied less upon what the Oracles said and more upon where my intuition was taking me, and time after time, when my intuition said something different to the Oracles, it was my intuition that was right.

It soon became clear that these Oracles simply opened doors, they should not be taken literally, their function was to take me to a particular place, to a state of mind where the right information would come.

With the I Ching, I would throw three coins, and the combinations of heads and tails would point me to a reading for guidance on my issue. In the I Ching there are 64 readings. I saw these as 64 rooms, and the coins were the doors that opened the rooms.

Once my imagination was in those rooms, information would come to me; often very specific information about my client would come to me. I felt that behind the scenes I was engaged in a dialogue, not in conversation, but in imagination.

I learned to have great faith in the information that came to me. Sometimes the story I wrote for a client did not seem to fit them when we met face to face. But the story always told the truth, and my clients would open up, to tell me what was going on behind the scenes.

On one occasion, in the reading I prepared, I wrote that my client was not in love with her husband, and that she had a secret life with another long-term relationship. I went on to write that so much of her life was a pretence, and that it was time she opened up to tell the truth. I knew nothing of this woman when I wrote her story, all I had was her name and address, and a very brief conversation to confirm the date for my visit. When I arrived at her house, I was struck by how idyllic it all was there, and how honest, happy and comfortable she seemed to be. I thought this time I must have got it wrong, and nervously I read her the story that I had prepared. She looked right through me until I had finished. I felt apologetic, but said nothing, and then she broke the silence, and she broke down in tears, and told me that what I had written was true. On one occasion, I prepared my reading without the full address; I had the street name, but not the house number. When I arrived, it was a very long street, and I wondered if I could pick out the house from the reading I had done.

In my reading, I wrote that the husband was very controlling, a perfectionist, and that the HEAVEN element was out of balance. Driving up the road I came to a house where a tall hedge had been neatly trimmed like a castle wall with a castellated top. I thought this must be the house, and of course it was.

Another time I arrived at the client's house having prepared a reading for someone of a different name, even so, the reading was correct.

I have long since let go of the need to have something tangible to link me with the client. The creative intelligence that works through the imagination seems to override any literal mistakes.

I used to allow my imagination to find its own way into the story of a client's life, but that was a long process, taking a lot of focus and energy. I have spent years finding a short cut. Now the Glass Runes and the homesouls readings at the end of this book are all I need. They bring clarity and focus to issues; they limit the field of possibilities, and direct the attention to the right place in the home. The imagination then takes over, and a wonderful journey begins.

So this book has been written as a self-help guide, for clients to continue to do the work without my help, and for lots more people to take a look at their homes in a new and rewarding way.

There are many ways to access the unknown. The Chinese used to read the I Ching by dividing bundles of yarrow stalks. Viking Runes were symbols marked on stone, and Celtic Druids used to read patterns in the formation of clouds and birds in flight. Perhaps the homesouls way is the modern way, more in tune with our psychology, more accessible and more legible to us. I know that many of my students have found it difficult to interpret the I Ching in relation to the home; its language is so foreign and its culture so different from ours.

The Invisible Plan and the Glass Runes evolved through my experience, to become a simple map and compass, to navigate the story of life within the home. With these tools, the home itself becomes a living oracle, so we each have a personal map, and a personal guide to find our way behind the scenes and to make a difference in our lives.

Rolled up paper or anything else marked with the nine colours or the nine elements can be used as a substitute for the Glass

Runes. It does not really matter what you use, but my personal preference is for glass. Glass is solid yet transparent, there, but not there, a portal for vision, an in between place, that is no place at all. It is the perfect material as a metaphor for soul.

In Welsh mythology there is a story, a precursor to the Arthurian tails of the quest for the Holy Grail. It is the story of Arthur's quest into the Otherworld to capture the pearl-rimmed cauldron that nourishes mortal life. This was the greatest treasure known to man, warmed by the breath of nine priestesses, a provider of plenty, and an Oracle of prophesy.

The quest for the cauldron was an arduous journey across the great water and into the unknown; a journey to a castle not of this world, 'a glass castle', perhaps beneath the sea, or in the starry skies to the north. This was Arianrhod's castle, the queen amongst priestesses. She was Ariadne to the Cretans, whose lover was Theseus, she who gave Theseus a lifeline, so that he could find his way back through the trials of the Labyrinth. None but Theseus returned from the Cretan labyrinth, and only seven men with Arthur returned from the glass castle.

Perhaps in truth, we are in the castle, living within the walls of glass, trapped in the labyrinth of life, between the ocean and the sky, ending our days in forgetfulness. Then one by one we remember, to awaken from a dreamy state, to find the line that tracks a way to the other side – the memory line, the story line, a thread that weaves its way through the web, back to the centre, to where the story first began.

There are many ways through the looking glass, and the castle has many doors. Through which one shall we journey to find what we are looking for?

The quest for the Grail begins with the question: What Ails Thee? And the Oracle at Delphi replies: Know Thyself!

Go to where the discomfort is. Pearls become beautiful because oysters deal with the discomfort that enters their space. When something irritating enters the oyster, the oyster deals with it in the way that oysters do – the result is a beautiful pearl.

The nine Glass Runes are pearls of wisdom, doors to

perception, through which we dialogue with the archetypal forces that shape our lives.

Creative force

The Secret of Home will guide you to explore the hidden landscape of your home and the deeper aspects of your life. There is a force behind this movement, the Chinese call it 'Chi', the Japanese call it 'KI', and the Welsh poet Dylan Thomas called it "*the force that through the green fuse drives the flower*". I simply think of it as 'Creative'. This force drives the life within the body, the feelings of the heart and the thoughts within the mind, but who can say from where this force has come?

Many wise people have given its source a name, and some have described its face. Some have called it God, but even God means different things to different people. The Author Julia Cameron in her book *The Artist Way* defines God as the force of Good Orderly Direction or flow; a creative and guiding force for all of us. It is sufficient to believe that The Glass Runes speak for themselves, and when we accept them as helpful guides they speak to us with a voice of guiding wisdom and authority, they help us to take a wider view. So when it seems that the homesouls Oracle readings are not answering your question directly, take a step back from the issue and take a wider view.

The Secret of Home will help you pay attention to your surroundings and to the quality of each passing moment. It will guide you to work with your spiritual calling and to bring this calling down to earth. The force that through the green fuse drives the flower drives your daily life and is ever present within the qualities of your home.

Be creative and flexible in the way you use the Glass Runes. Trust your intuition. At first you may take what is written in the readings literally, but in time you will develop deeper understanding and a more personal relationship with each Rune.

Your Runes themselves are common items designed for ornamental use around the home, but when you decide to work with the Secret of Home they become tools for engaging your imagination, opening doors into intuitive realms from which the information you need will flow. Intuitively you may know what area of the home to work on – you may even be working on it already.

If you don't have a question, just use the homesouls readings to familiarise yourself with the qualities of the plan. Do the work, make your changes, and note what happens, and in time you will become well acquainted with how the different areas of your home affect aspects of your life. The Glass Runes inhabit a space where there is no distinction between fiction and fact, a space where the imagination has healing power. Use them to guide your imagination to find the story of your life within your home. When the imagination is engaged within the home, the healing process begins. Then the story, the teller, and the place all receive healing.

Entering the wound

Your home is a living oracle, it holds the story of your life.

You are its author, the caller and the called, not the one who plans its course from beginning through to end, but the one who goes with its flow, navigating, exploring and discovering, nourishing your story along its way.

Nourish the space within your home as if you are nourishing your life as a whole.

What does your home tell you?

What is its Calling?

How might it help you?

Our homes are vessels that carry us through the invisible

landscape. The Invisible Plan is the map, and The Glass Runes are like stars helping us to navigate the way. The quest is to find contentment simply to be at home in our lives. The method is simple and light, encouraging us to make light of our situations and to become lighter in our way of being in the world.

The interior landscape of home is a dreamscape, there is more here than meets the eye: the way each room is arranged, the way each room is used, and the artefacts on the walls and in the cabinets offer a lot to the imagination.

The Secret of Home is a psychology of home, a new field of enquiry for which there is no established language.

Feng Shui which has its roots in China, is the only model, yet the Secret of Home is not like Feng Shui, because it does not look at the home for the causes of life's problems, but sees the home as a reflection of the way things are. Problems in the home are necessary; actually they are treasures, for they call to us for transformation.

Our homes do not govern our fate, they simply mirror to us the way we are being and the way we are going. They call to us and we can call back and change the way things are, for we are authors of our own life stories.

Feng Shui has been lifted out of context. Yes, its Soul is universal, but its spirit is Oriental. It has come to the West and we have cleaned it up, with chimes and flowers, and scented candles. We call in the master, we read the books and we become enlightened. Yes, it works here, but what work does it do, and at what cost does it do the work? Its language is curative, if you have a problem you look to solve it by finding the right cure. This is out of context for us now.

Archetypal psychology and complementary health look at a symptom as something symbolic or metaphoric going on in the bigger picture of a person's life.

We enter the wound, to find the opportunity in the problem, to see through it rather than transcend it. Feng Shui deflates the value of a problem by treating it as a sickness that needs a cure.

The fantasy of the sick building relies upon the expert for prognosis and healing, then the client/resident becomes dependent upon their help, and is at a loss when they are not around – only he can help me, for only he knows what is wrong.

Feng Shui translated means: "Wind and Water," but we are not engaged within its story, we stand outside looking in, inspired but not empowered. Its cures are like chemical tablets: we need the right thing in the right place, because the wrong thing in the wrong place will harm our lives.

This idea has not journeyed well into the Western Psyche. We have flavoured it, but it does not really fit.

James Hillman in his book *Revisioning Psychology*, says: "*We owe our symptoms an immense debt. The soul can exist without its therapists but not without its afflictions*". The symptom is a symbol through which we enter the story. The problem or the wound presents us with the image. We need the image as an invitation to enter, to stand under in order to understand, to deconstruct. This is the drama in the theatre, the arena in which we become Soul makers.

When a wound becomes part of your identity, you are trapped within the prison of your story. There are many ways to be imprisoned within a story. Here are some that I have heard:

- *I hate my job, but at least it provides security.*
- *I do not love him, but I cannot leave him.*
- *If I do things differently I will be worse off.*
- *Someone else is to blame for the way my life is.*
- *There is nothing I can do about it.*
- *This is the way it is supposed to be.*
- *I cannot help the way I am.*

These negative images are wounds -- they are symptoms, symbolic of what is happening behind the scenes. If you are in one, stand back and take a look at it, follow its story line. Where is its image in your home? What is your home saying about the issue? Work on the image as a way to work behind the scenes. Things will change, and you have to be awake to follow the changes, to keep track of what is happening, to get to know more about the deeper aspects of who you are.

In the earlier story of Arthur's quest for the Grail/ the Cauldron of Plenty, I failed to mention something that was written by the Welsh Bard Taliesen. In the poem *'Preiddeu Annwn'*, written by him in the fourteenth century, he said of the Cauldron: "*Ny beirw bwyt llwfyr ny rytyghit*" meaning: "*It does not boil the food of a coward; it is not destined. It serves only the courageous*".

Fear of change is one of the greatest fears that people have. Often people identify with their wounds, in a wounded condition they can become the centre of attention. The language of wounds is now at home in the human condition; well at least in the conditions of so many people that I have met. So many people inhabit their wounds, inviting people into the arena of their wounded story, drawing comfort from the attention. Emotionally we are all cut and bruised, and from time to time we nurse the ego. But entering the wound is an act of courage, a crossing of a threshold, an exploration, a vision quest, not an invitation to a pity party, where we exchange our sad life stories. When next you catch yourself becoming a reflection of a sad life story, just ask yourself, how much are you at home within this image. If you cannot live without this wound, at least be honest, if only to yourself, and if you feel that you do not belong there, then exercise the power to be the author of your own life story.

Often we define ourselves by the work we do and the careers we choose, by the house we live in and what we have, the people we associate with, the conditions of our health, and the things we talk about. But these are only outward expressions of a story we believe to be true, they are not the whole person and the whole life, only images of one's identity.

We all want to set right what is wrong with our lives, but outward appearances are not the root of our problems. They serve only to illuminate the symptoms, and are symbolic of what needs to change. They mirror to us our internal conflicts and lay bare our wounds as an invitation to see more clearly what is holding us back.

So always there is one big question: What Ails Thee? And always there is one answer: Know Thyself!

When you move into soulless territory, you can feel it. There is a numbing of the senses, the feeling that you have moved over to automatic pilot, the lights are on, but you are not really at home.

Life does this to us all at times, but many people live continuously in this state. It is not a catatonic state, because to outside appearances everything is functioning as normal. Life without animation, without mystery and magic, will do this to us. I lost it for a few years, working in a big office 8 till 5 and lots, lots more: lots of pressure, lots of responsibility, plenty of money, and not enough of a life.

I walked the corridors as an architect, between the engineers, the quantity surveyors, the interior designers and the secretaries.

I longed for the space and time to dream a little, to let my mind wander, to shower in the mystery of life. How many people are out there walking those corridors still?

It may not be right to leave, everyone has their own path to tread, but paths that lack in Soul are too short and too narrow. If this is so for you, your scene may not need to change as mine did, but the way you place yourself within it could give everything a new perspective.

Fixed images with literal meanings have become idols in a modern day perspective. Everything can be taken literally, and so often it is. Change the context – see through different eyes, look in a way that you have not looked before, and what was once so vacuous and dull is now so bright and full of mystery.

Taking things literally has become a form of worship, in order to have faith one must be in full possession of the facts, to have a realistic approach towards problem solving, one must be given data that can be relied upon. Calculating, measuring and anticipating the outcome "as if" we are in control, "as if" this is the only way to achieve what we want in life.

In this narrow corridor of vision, there is little room for inspiration, the ground is not fertile for creativity and there is little delight for Soul to walk this way. In the theatre of the Soul there are so many doors. But which one will lead to Heaven on this Earth? We choose. We have this much authority. We open and life enters. One man sees a valley filled with tears, another sees a valley filled with soul, while others do not see, they do not pause, they race headlong, blinkered, one behind the other, entering the human race, vying for position, as if it really matters.

This book opens a door for you to see your home in a new way, to enter each space as if you were entering a new territory, as if you were walking through the theatre of your Soul. And if you think you are too old, or too wise for this fantasy, then close the door and walk away. For this is a journey requiring imagination, not a self build course, not a course for personal development, but a course in de-construction, a course that will take you behind the scenes to look at how you have built your life around your story.

Maybe you have walked through the vale of tears, maybe you have run the gauntlet through the valley, maybe you are weary from the race, or just plain curious. Then begin to see your home as a mirror of your life filled with images that reflect the calling of your Soul. Each day images call you, and each day you have passed them by.

Now it is time to take a look, paying attention to what is happening behind the scenes, seeing the valley as a place of nourishment, to pause, take a look around, and recognise that Soul is in the making.

The poet John Keats, once wrote in a letter to his brother: "*Call the world if you please, 'the vale of soul making'... How then are souls to be made? ...How but by the medium of a world like this.*"

Our vulnerabilities and wounds, dreams and aspirations, destiny and life's calling, all show up in the details of our homes. So we can turn to our homes for support to heal the issues in our lives, to call for what we want, and to discover what is meant to be. This requires an insightful way of looking, not being fooled by appearances or literal impressions, but seeing things symbolically, knowing that everything tells a story and anything could be the key you need to solve a mystery.

You can discover so much about your life by considering the context in which the things that matter to you are placed. I don't just mean the physical environment that surrounds them, but where, when and how they occur in your story and in the emotional landscape of your life.

For instance, consider a picture on your wall: Why did you place it on that wall? Who gave it to you? What does it mean to you? How does it make you feel? The room and the wall that hold your picture also hold a part of your life story. Your picture in this context becomes a symptom and a symbol of things that happen in your life. The picture tells a story far more significant than what appears within its frame.

The story of Esther and Hylas

Whenever I visit my friend Esther she is in the bath. She loves the bath, and being a single parent with four children living at home, the bathroom is her sanctuary.

I recall a couple of years ago wondering what the relationship between her bathroom and the bigger picture of her life might be, so I gave her something to think about.

I told her that her bathroom was in the EARTH area of her house, and that this area holds issues about relationships and motherhood. I asked her to contemplate this the next time she had a bath. Well, the next time I called she had been soaking in the atmosphere of the bathroom and thinking about her relationships with her children and their fathers, but I had an inkling that she had not gone deeply enough into her story. So I took a look myself.

Her house was formerly the village police station, and her bathroom was the old prison cell. Steel bars on the small window took me back to the time when the room was not so cosy, not a

 sanctuary but a jail room. At a low level next to the toilet, was a picture, obviously placed there so she could look at it from the bath. I was intrigued, for me it seemed to say so much. I asked her to

contemplate the picture and to consider its presence in this sanctuary that was once a prison cell.

The next time I called, Esther had plenty to say about the picture. Her story line was that the men in her life would not give her what she wanted. In the picture it seemed to her the woman was trying to coax the man into the water, but he would not go in. And yet in this picture there are so many other possible points of view. From a male perspective, the image might seem like a dream come true – seven naked women – all of them inviting the man in. Is this a scene of enchantment, or is it entrapment? How would you read the scene? There are so many possibilities, What we see in it and the things we choose not to see, tell us so much about the way we are, and the way that our life is.

The painting, by John William Waterhouse, is called *Hylas and the Nymphs*. The story is that of a young man called Hylas, he sailed with Jason and the Argonauts in search of the Golden Fleece. This painting depicts the place where Hylas departs the scene. He set off to find fresh drinking water, but he found. more than he bargained for. As painted by John William Waterhouse, the myth becomes an evocation of feminine guile and sensuality. Hylas is drawn in by the allure of the femme fatale, never to be seen again. His fate is left to our imagination, could it be an abrupt death by drowning or everlasting sexual bliss?

What quality has this place, is it Womb or Tomb? The painting begs this question. For Esther it is a womb, a watery sanctuary, yet something harks back to the time when the bathroom was a place of incarceration. Esther has the freedom to open the door, but history is still visible through the window. Prison bars on the inside, a graveyard filled with tombstones on the outside, this gives her story a darker context, an unusual setting for such a comforting sanctuary.

When you take a deeper look at your home, you take a deeper look at your self.

"Your vision is your home. A closed vision always wants to make a small room out of whatever it sees. Thinking that limits you denies your life. In order to deconstruct the inner prison the first step is learning to see that it is a prison. You can move in the direction of this discovery by reflecting on the places where your life feels limited and tight. To recognise the crippling feeling of being limited is already to have begun moving beyond it… To be free is nothing, to become free is everything."
John O'Donohue

I visited Esther this morning, to catch up on her latest news. True to form she had just got out of the bath, and so I asked, what is the big thing about you and the bath? She said, *"It is so deeply cleansing, it is something about being immersed in the water, it is like a new start to each day."* She drifted, it was early and she had not had the customary shot of coffee to wake her to the day. Then, as if jolted into wakefulness, now looking angry and upset, she said, *"but there are still those f…ing bars on the window, it is still a prison"*.

Before I tell you what has come to the surface, I had better fill in a bit more background. Esther is a single parent, she has four children by three fathers, and all four children live with her in a rented house. The fathers are not entirely absent, but they are hardly ever there for the children. This story is about the wound that Esther has entered, it is a love story with a number of twists, and it is too soon to know what the outcome will be. The story takes us into three Scenes in Esther's life:

Scene 2. Earth
Being a woman. Being a mother. Wanting a good husband. Wanting a home of her own.

Scene 7. Lake
Abandonment. Entrapment. Abuse. The loss of innocence.

Scene 6. Heaven
Absent Fathers. The romantic view. Making choices.

Esther is now back together with Hylas number 1, her first love of 21 years ago. But how did she get here in this picture, and what happened to Hylas in the picture during this time? This is her story: They were young then, unable to commit, for both had plans for the future. They put some distance between each other, but remained good friends, providing for each other a safe place to harbour in times of need.

When Esther moved on from her first love, she met another. This time she was ready, she wanted this man, but he was not the settling down type. Let's call him Hylas number 2. I don't need to give you the literal details, just look at the image in the picture. This Hylas is kneeling on the bank of the lake looking adoringly at Esther as she bathes herself in the water. Esther wanted him, she beguiled him, she tempted him, and she tried to pull him in, but he was not willing. She wanted him so much she thought the way to trap him was to become pregnant and to have his baby. It did not work, he was a wanderer so he moved on, and she was heart-broken, at home alone with her first baby. When Hylas number 3 entered the scene, Esther was very vulnerable, she had been single for a long time. This time it was this man's physical beauty that attracted her, she fell in love with the way he looked, she did not look much deeper, she dived straight in, not thinking what the consequences might be. She had two children by this man with whom she was not suited. When Hylas number 4 appeared upon the scene, he was so many things that number 2 and number 3 were not. He was very small, where the other two were very tall. He was for a short while a good companion, but 'more like a child than a man', so she said. She provided so many things that he did not have: a house, a family, security, someone to care for him, but when he got all of this, it became the opposite of what he wanted. This Hylas, unlike number 2, did not walk away. Like Hylas number 3 he entered the water, but he saw it as a trap, he saw himself as a prisoner in this house, and a prisoner of Esther's circumstances. He accused her of trapping him with all the things that she could offer, and again she got pregnant, but this was not the man she wanted either.

So where did it all begin? *"I lost my innocence in my childhood, when my father abandoned me. He left me in a world of adults, where my stepfather emotionally tortured me, and I went to an all girls' school, so I did not have any male role models. I have since been looking for stability, but looking to males who cannot provide this for me. Also I did not believe I was worthy of this."*

HEAVEN – Where is the Father?

A few years ago, at a time when Esther was in a deep emotional crisis, she turned to the Landmark Forum, to help her uncover and examine what was holding her back in her life. After one of the meetings she went up to the facilitator and asked for some advice. She told her story in a nutshell, and the facilitator's advice was: *Get the absent fathers out of your life.* I am not going to add anything about the quality of that advice, it was what she wanted to hear, and it helped her. What I will say is if you look at the plan of her home as a picture of her life, the fathers are not in that picture. The HEAVEN area relates to Fathers, and it is missing from Esther's house plan.

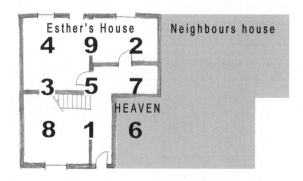

In Esther's house the HEAVEN area is actually part of the house next door. The people next door help Esther a lot; they look after the children, and they help her in all sorts of other ways. Once they even tried to buy her house from the landlord so they could provide her with more security. So there is help and support for her in many ways, she has lots of good friends, but the support does not come from the fathers. You may well ask at this point, what other qualities live within this area of her life, what else is missing, or what other qualities may need some integration to make her life more whole.

I am not suggesting that everyone with the HEAVEN area missing have the same issues, nothing I say should be taken that literally, everything should be considered within its particular context. Other issues might be: Judgement, Religion, Communication. Perhaps it would be helpful to refer to the list of keywords in Chapter 2, Scene 6. Other issues that I think are particularly relevant here for Esther are Perfectionism and Romanticism. Esther says of her father, *"He was always the most desirable man for me. He was the one I wanted to impress, but he was so hard to please, he was always dismissive of how well I was doing, he always wanted me to do better. I never knew how to be good enough to have a man who really valued me. My Father was the root of my relationship problems with men, and my low self esteem."*

Esther is a romantic, she longs for what she does not have, and she holds an ideal of what this is. She continues to be hard on herself, never living up to the ideal of what she could be, making comparisons with other women who are better off, have more of what they want, are more attractive, and more appreciated. She has an ideal notion of how she should be, and how she would like her man to be. Perhaps her vision is not unrealistic; it is certainly romantic and idealistic. In her romantic notion about her life, this house is where she would settle with her perfect man and all their children, and they would also own the house next door, so this would be their perfect house.

She put the painting up in the loft for a few months, not knowing what else to do with it, out of sight was out of mind, but the issues did not go away. Perhaps she was placing it in the lap of the gods, I should rephrase that: perhaps being a Christian she was handing the issue over to God. Praying for the man she wanted, she made the specific request that he should be 'a good Christian'. It was not long before her prayer was answered, quite literally – his name was 'Christian'. She fell deeply in love with him, he was a strong man, tall, dark and handsome, he was well grounded and could provide stability and security for Esther and the children. But there were complications – he was already married. Esther felt his love was true, and his marriage was already on the rocks, it had been for some time, so they made commitments to each other. But in the end, he could not break his vows to his wife. Esther was again left broken hearted, feeling unworthy, unloved and alone.

Her prayer for what she wanted was answered, she wanted a good Christian, and that is what she got, he was a good man, whose name was 'Christian', but he was not available. Perhaps we could take this as a lesson, to be clear about what we wish for. There are so many choices, and sometimes what we desire becomes a reaction to what we have already had, based on knowing what we do not want. The ability to make good choices concerning men is not a faculty Esther considers she is blessed with.

If Scene 6 in the plan was to have another name, instead of HEAVEN I would call it 'Boundaries', or better still 'Choices'. Finding our Heaven on Earth, or making our Heaven on Earth, is determined by the choices that we make – we have this much authority.

Some may decide to *live more in the flow*, so they choose to *let go* of making so many choices. I want to overstate this as a paradox, because to go with the flow is still a choice, and in the flow there are still so many choices and judgements to be made. 'Choices' are held within the HEAVEN area of the plan, they share the space with 'Calling' – at least that is what I believe.

I believe that we are 'Called'. We have a destiny, there is a sacred plan, but Heaven on this Earth is built upon the choices that we make.

Here we perceive the walls that surround us, we envision our own reality, we build our lives structured on our beliefs, so HEAVEN is the place of religious convictions, and scientific points of view, of the judgements that we make. It is the place where we take the role of Editor, editing our real life scripts.

Whatever we choose to believe sets the scene for the way that our world will be. HEAVEN is not an element that takes us out into the world, it is more to do with boundaries, and it is the place through which we structure our own realities.

It is through THUNDER that we enter the drama of the world, especially along the storyline between THUNDER and LAKE, along this line there is always so much drama. (For an example of the relationship between Thunder and Lake read: 'Diana's story' in Chapter 3 – Reading your home).

"All the world's a stage, And all the men and women merely players..."

This is what Shakespeare wrote – and I think it is so. We decide the extent to which our lives are blessed or limited and the potential we have for love and happiness.

Earth is the stage upon which we make our home. EARTH is matter and mother, it can be both Womb and Tomb, there is a subtle difference in the structure of the words, but a world of difference in the structure of the experience.

The beliefs upon which we structure our lives, and the choices that we make, determine the way in which our lives are bounded.

Esther said to me, *"all relationships can be a womb or tomb, it just depends how you feel about it at the time."* And this morning in her bath, looking at the bars on the window, once again she felt like it was a prison.

When the relationship with Christian was over Esther brought the painting out of the loft to take a closer look at what she was dealing with. Thinking about the way she has been hurt, she said, *"I come across as so strong, but my strength is brittle, it can easily be destroyed by people who want to see through it, or break it down. The other side of this strength is to be truly and honestly vulnerable."* She thought this might be her answer, citing an inspiration from the Bible, that God said, *"come to me as an innocent – be as innocent as a lamb and you will have everything".*

LAKE is the place of 'Innocence' in the plan, so this is where Esther decided to put the painting. She hung it on the wall facing the bathroom door so that when the door was open the light through the prison window shone upon the painting.

Esther knew there was an issue about entrapment, she had set a trap for Hylas number 2 by becoming pregnant, and she was accused of trapping Hylas number 4, although this was not her intention. Her motivation for placing the painting in LAKE was clear; she wanted to address issues about vulnerability, innocence and entrapment, she wanted to reclaim her innocence in relation-ships.

One day with the bathroom door wide open and the light beaming through the prison window, she focussed on the painting in a new way.

"I noticed the lily in the central nymphs hair, and I realised that I am

the centre - that woman in the water became me. I realised it was up to me to find my man, and I was no longer one of many over forty and dead in the water. I am complicated - I am all seven women in the water. I am looking at the man and saying you can have all of me, all of these aspects of me, but you have to plunge in, you are not going to have a fully immersed relationship with me until you can accept all of these aspects of who I am".

Once again Esther's call was answered, perhaps this one is the love of her life. "*He has been there all the time, he was my first love and we have been friends for 21 years. He says he truly loves me and he will never let me go.*" He proposed, and she accepted. This is Hylas number 1, after all this time, and now they are going to be married – or are they? There are complications. There is another woman in the water, Hylas number 1 has been married before and he is still great friends with his ex wife – she does not want to let him go, and the further into the water Esther and Hylas go, the more obstacles they find that are in the way. Esther said to me, "*I don't see the issue any more as being in the painting, I see it as being the prison bars, and there is nothing I can do about them, because I rent the place.*"

In reply I quoted John O'Donohue again: "*In order to deconstruct the inner prison the first step is learning to see that it is a prison. You can move in the direction of this discovery by reflecting on the places where your life feels limited and tight.*"

If Esther and Hylas find the courage to make the journey into the water together, both of them being honest, open and vulnerable, then perhaps they will discover truth in what John O'Donohue said: "*To recognise the crippling feeling of being limited is already to have begun moving beyond it... To be free is nothing, to become free is everything.*"

There are two key points I want to make about Esther's house:

1. **In EARTH -** Esther is not allowed to remove the prison bars from the window.
2. **In HEAVEN -** There is nothing she can do about owning the Heaven area.

These are not just injuries or afflictions, these are very deep wounds. Some might say, just move, go and find another house. This would not be my advice – this will not work, these issues are too deep, they will resurface in another place at another time. In this place, these wounds are wide open, and Esther has the courage to enter them here. It is not easy for her, and she is not at a time in her story where she can see a happy ending. But the opportunity is here for Esther and Hylas, I wonder if they will take it?

I have given you this story because I wanted to take you right into the middle of a difficult scene, just to show you what I mean by finding the image, entering the wound, and deconstructing the inner prison. I will give you plenty of stories with happy endings, but this one informs what it can be like in the middle of the story. I am very grateful to Esther, for having the courage to allow us to look so closely at her wound.

One last thing, perhaps a further twist, or maybe another point of view:

What about the other women?

With all these men there have been several other women in the picture. Esther sees the picture as several aspects of herself, but it can also be read as several other women in the water with her. So who are these women? I think she knows them all. So follow my lead just for the moment as I pick up the thread of this storyline.

The HEAVEN area is missing, and for a few years Esther has been aware of some issues here: Absent Fathers, Control, Limitations, Boundaries. All she had of the HEAVEN area in her house was the inside of its boundary wall. So it is this wall that she has been working on in an attempt to integrate HEAVEN more into her life. And she has seen significant results. Again she has focussed her intent into a painting on the wall.

The first time she did this, her intention was to draw Hylas number 2, number 3, and number 4, closer to her and the children, for them to be better fathers and to give her more support, It worked for a while.

Another time she felt insecure because her landlord was considering moving back into the rented house. This brought up issues about the landlord (a man), having too much control over her life, so she started to look for another house, and she did something about the control issue by changing a painting on the HEAVEN wall. On changing the painting, the landlord ceased to be so obstructive; he softened, and offered to sell the rented house to her. She did not have the money to buy it, but friends came forward who could buy it as an investment for themselves, and this would give her the security she needed. Actually it did not work out, because the landlord changed his mind about selling the house.

This HEAVEN wall is significant, and always her focus has been on a painting, so here is the twist that I could see when I visited her.

Hylas number 1 was married to an artist, a good painter, who Esther really admired. When Hylas number 1 and Esther were just good friends, his wife the artist gave Esther a painting that she hung upon the HEAVEN wall. This painting hung upon the wall for a long time, until Esther came on one of my courses.

She saw this as a powerful painting that could help her in the THUNDER area of her life (at this time there was nothing other than friendship between Esther and Hylas number 1).

Then another good friend painted a picture for her that she placed on the HEAVEN wall, to replace the picture from the wife of Hylas number 1. This friend and painter happens to be the lover of Hylas number 3.

So looking at this boundary wall to the HEAVEN area from another perspective, it is possible to see so many connections to Hylas and the other women (the wives and the lovers), in the story of this wall.

So this is where I will leave Esther's story.

Living in your story

Your home holds your whole life story. Everything about you lives somewhere in your home. Your home is an expression of your sorrows and your joys, your self-esteem and other people's influences, health, wealth and relationships, desires, ambitions, boundaries, and your radiance.

Just as a single cell can tell a story about the whole organism, and the tongue, eyes and feet can be used for diagnosing illness in the whole body, so all the details of the home reflect the way things are in our lives.

All you need to know is close at hand right now, certainly within your field of vision. If you look around and cannot see this, it is because there is another way of looking, a way that you can begin to learn here if you want to know so much more about the magic of your own life.

What separates you from the magic is an illusion, a thin veil drawn across everything you can see.

We believe that we are awake and walking in a world where we see most clearly, but we are not fully conscious, we mistake illusion for reality, believing all that we can see to be true and not realising the extent to which we deceive ourselves. We must train ourselves to see beyond the facades, for our bodies tell another story, the things we surround ourselves with have so much hidden meaning, and our homes are intimately connected with the whole of our lives.

> *"To see the world in a grain of sand, and to see heaven in a wild flower,*
> *hold infinity in the palm of your hands, and eternity in an hour."*
>
> William Blake

Everything there is to know about space and time could be perceived in a simple grain of sand if only we knew how to see it. Perhaps a tall order, too much for anyone to comprehend in its wholeness, but we might at least catch an occasional glimpse of the infinite space for some of the time.

The homesouls Oracle will meet you at the threshold. You must open your eyes and ask the right question, and then a door will open to pierce the veil. Life in its fullness opens to you when you decide to go there.

If for one moment you draw back and ask what sense can there be in all this, then pause for that moment to consider what Albert Einstein once said, *"logic can take you from A to B, but imagination encircles the world"*.

In your home The Glass Runes will take you to point B, where you will stand at the threshold of the imagination. This is indeed another nation, an invisible landscape, uncharted territory, the space where everything is whole, but nothing can be measured. It is where we all meet in our collective unconscious, and where we travel in our dreams. Albert Einstein, William Blake and all the others we consider inspired with genius, have pierced the veil and brought into this world the things we need to know. But we misunderstand, misinterpret and often blunder our way through our lives.

It is time for all to find their genius, and to do it not just for ourselves, but as a gift to the world. We are all connected and so we all share the same wounds. Our personal scars run deep and affect the hidden landscape we all share. What we do for ourselves to heal our own wounds, we do for all and we heal our planet.

Life is a journey of discovery, to find our way home, to feel content, and to know that we belong. As we walk in the valleys of our lives, we meet our own shadows, the parts of ourselves we try to disown or lock away in places we don't want to visit.

The homesouls Journey will help you recover your strength and resolve to live a better life, to confront your shadows and remove the masks that hide your wounds, to explore the places in your life that are not filled with grace.

We all wear masks to shield our vulnerabilities, they are the images we project into the world. Some say, "I am hard, so don't come near me," or "I am weak, please protect me," and "I am a victim, poor me." Or they say, "I am so clever, you will never catch me out," or "I am desirable, see how sexy I look."

We masquerade on the stage upon which we set ourselves, thinking it is the life we deserve. And what we project into the world is reflected back to us. How we see the world becomes who we are and what we experience in the world is a reflection of what we become.

The mind constructs a story that the ego feels comfortable to live with. That is why we must look beyond the way things appear to be if we are to know the truth about any situation,

A mechanical object without a

My daughter Charlotte age 12 and her drawing inspired by Picasso

heart and without a mind can be programmed to reach its final destination on time. But it is the heart and the mind that navigate our way. When they are incongruent, we worry where life is headed. We arrive, look back, and wonder where we have been, and what we have lost along the way.

Some say: *'If only I had my time over again'*, *'If only I were more attractive... more intelligent... had more money...'*

'If only' becomes part of our biography, sometimes a melancholy moan that fosters discontent and holds us back, and sometimes a wake-up call saying something must be done. Our longing is a heartfelt calling of the Soul, it moves us to find our way home, for belonging has nest-like qualities, it calls from the bosom of mothers and the arms of lovers. It calls from the hearth fires, where we can find peace to be at home with ourselves.

Life receives us into its fold, and from our joy and pain flow tears that pave the way to hidden treasures. I am talking not only of tears that fall like rain, for then there would be little hope for so many who find it hard to cry, but especially of the hidden tears, those that fall behind our eyes to form a lake inside; the lake of 'Hiraeth' that longs to be fulfilled.

You have great waters to cross, mountains to climb, dark and cavernous depths to descend. Follow your creative light to find your way through this inner landscape. It is this light that ignites your heart to love and the hearth fires to welcome you home, illuminating the darkest places of your melancholy, anger, desperation and pain. It is this light that will bring comfort in your darkest nights. It is a promise on the horizon and a light of hope that calls you to journey.

When you walk in this light, life is not just amusing, pleasant and happy but scintillating. This light is your Scintilla (your inner genius), like the Olympic flame, it calls you to reach your highest potential, transcending the barriers of pain and defeat to do the best you can in the human race.

Your inner genius longs for the freedom to be creative, to dream and to play. Yet some people keep it bottled up, not realizing their hidden potential, not expressing what they truly feel.

We all have genius, for it is through genius that we perceive the world in the mirror of our lives, in the faces and the actions of other people and in the places, the things and the spaces that surround us. Genius accompanies us in our lives, it can find the higher path, and it calls to us from beyond the mirror. It says to us:

Change your view and your experience will change too.

Soul animates everything that matters in your life so that you may realise your potential to be radiant, wonderful, and truly alive. It stirs the cauldron of tears and cooks the broth, mixing the ingredients of life's story so you will be nourished. It alerts you to what you need to know; to become wise by trusting your instincts, gaining insight and learning from intuition.

So follow your nose to find the right trail home, with the inspiration to see your problems as opportunities in disguise and to find creative solutions for your healing.

We are all homesouls searching for home; dwellers on the threshold, longing for what is missing in our lives, looking for happiness, to feel less pain and close the gap on separation. Our longing drives us home, burning in the heart, and as we get closer the longing eases and the heart feels content.

Our true home is not a place around us but a space within us. We sometimes feel it as an emptiness that needs to be filled, but it is not empty, it is always filled with the whole presence of our lives.

What we experience on the outside is a reflection of that inner space. To be at home in oneself we must also be at home in the spaces we inhabit- in the body, the identity and the living environment. Soul longs to be at home in these places. If life is to be a Soul full experience we must make ourselves at home in these places.

The house you live in is a theatre of Soul. It is the place where everything that matters comes home to roost, a sacred vessel into which you can look for inspiration, journey towards wisdom, and call for abundance and healing. It holds your whole life story and carries you through it. Every cupboard, every picture, book and ornament, the doors, windows, walls – every part of the fabric of your home says something about you, they are your biography, symbolic ingredients of your whole life story.

You need look no further for alchemy to begin. For within your home the mundane and the ordinary are both special and precious.

There's no place like home!

Chapter 2

Through the looking glass

A journey through the looking glass

"All the world's a stage, And all the men and women merely players..." so said Jaques in Shakespeare's *As You Like It.*

So we script our own life stories, stage by stage, we decide the extent to which our lives are blessed or limited, and the potential we have for love and happiness.

We are not alone in this endeavour, we share each scene with other people, and within each person's individuality, there are many characters at play.

Within my own life, so many characters play each scene. I am architect, storyteller, father, guide, child, warrior, and victim, to name just a few. These are my archetypes, they play away in the background of my story, they shape my identity, and they define my life.

Each of us has our archetypes. I think of archetypes as the architects of Soul, because we build our lives around concepts of who we are. Our archetypes have a creative role; they give our lives form. They connect the way we live, with the way it is behind the scenes.

They connect home with Soul. I am not going to say much more about the archetypes of identity – the major players upon the stage: Karl Jung, James Hillman, Caroline Myss and others, have said plenty about the archetypes.

I want to take you backstage, through the invisible landscape of the eight elements that exist within our homes. If the archetypes of our identities are the architects of Soul, then the eight elements are their architecture: WATER, MOUNTAIN, THUNDER, WIND, FIRE, EARTH, LAKE, HEAVEN. These elements animate our biography, biology, and living environment.

In relation to biology, they have been explored through Chinese Medicine, Acupuncture and Shiatsu. In relation to the built environment they have informed Feng Shui. With this book, I will now take you into a less explored territory, to see each element as a mirror of life, through which you can see your own story in the details of your home.

Here is a map with which we can explore the archetypal elements of change. For the purpose of this journey, I would like you to see this as a story map. It has eight scenes gathered around the centre, and each of us is in the audience at the centre looking at the scenes. As we enter each scene we

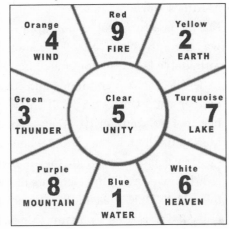

open a door to perceive the way our lives are through the particular quality of each place.

To locate the map within your home you will need to refer back to Chapter 1.

In writing the Secret of Home over the past eleven years, every question has led me somewhere, and when I was lacking under-standing, something relevant would come my way. I am not going to define the shape of this intelligence, I cannot do that, yet it seems to me there is a creative intelligence that plays away behind the scenes, that works a way through the imagination, and motions things towards us in life and home. This is my experience.

The homesouls journey is a journey into the imagination of home. Imagination is a doorway to Soul. Guidance is in every home for everyone, we just have to learn to read the signs. In every house there are signs, things that call for attention, that want to be discovered, that can take you deeper into your story so you can change the way things are in your life.

I have followed these signs through so many houses, helping each person to journey through their rooms as if journeying through the story of their life. So often when we look at something that at first appears to be so ordinary, a closer look reveals a deeply personal reflection. Every house is full of detail, and within every detail there is a story waiting to be told.

Martha's story:

Martha is a formidable lady approaching retirement age and she was recently bereaved of her mother, who was an even more formidable lady. She told me of her mother's controlling influence in her life, that her childhood and creativity had been stifled by her mother and even as an adult she was constantly undermined by her mother's authority. It was not until her mother died that Martha finally felt she could be herself.

This was the main theme in her life story, the issues were clearly linked with the elements of THUNDER and LAKE, and in the THUNDER area of her home the story played itself out. THUNDER relates to many things, but above all to issues of authority, to the conditions we allow to influence our lives, and to becoming the author of our own life stories.

A grand piano took pride of place in the THUNDER area, and on the piano there were old prints of fairy illustrations.

The magical world of children and fairies is very much to do with LAKE and the dialogue between THUNDER and LAKE often raises issues about one's self-esteem. I was keen to know the story. The piano, she said, was the one thing her mother encouraged her to play (her mother was a keen pianist).

The fairies were drawings of her mother as a child; she had posed as a model for the fairy in a well-known book. This was a revelation to us both: in this place of 'Authority' and 'Life's conditioning', her mother was represented as a fairy child.

This image of her mother had been far from Martha's imagination, but now she could see that what had become lost to her mother many years ago was also lost to her. Mother and daughter shared the same story and neither had seen the other in their own reflection. What had become stifled in Martha's life had also been stifled in her mother's life, and most likely in the generations before them.

Martha had found inspiration by looking at the area of THUNDER and she went on to express her own creativity and self-worth in the area of LAKE.

The Lake and the Well

When we turn to LAKE, more than any other element, LAKE holds the secrets and the mysteries of life. It is to the Lake that we must come to find the magic in our scenes, for often what we look for is not visible at the surface, we must journey deeper.

LAKE is the child within every adult, the imagination behind the picture, the joy behind the inspiration for life, and the potential within the idea. To journey into LAKE, is to enter the looking glass, to discover more about who we are. Whenever you hear a story about a Lake or a Well, consider its relevance to this area of your life and home.

In Wales we have many myths and legends that centre on the lakes and the wells. In Caitlin and John Mathews' book *Ladies of the Lake*, they tell a story of a far off time, before King Arthur. A time when Faery maidens, offered hospitality at the wells, giving freely to all travellers. Then came a time when a King called Amangons abused the hospitality of a maiden and the well. He raped her and stole her golden cup. Amangons's knights followed his lead, raping the other maidens at their wells. And so, the maidens withdrew from our land, and the land became impoverished.

And how impoverished is modern life, how clean is the water and how pure are our intentions. In the cut and thrust, hard sell, hard line of mainstream culture, how often do you find your way to the Lake, and what do you find there.

The Lake and the Well are not just filled with wishes and wellness. So many clients with issues in LAKE, have also experienced sexual abuse and child abuse. It is distressing to recall how many times I have been told of these experiences when looking at LAKE in client's homes. I wish it were not so. All forms of abuse that injure the spirit are called for healing to this place. But we don't care so much for it any more, the door is barely open, the wish is there but not the Will.

When a victim hangs his head in shame or guilt, this gesture harkens to the LAKE, *'I wish it were different'* – a call for innocence to be protected. In LAKE we are so vulnerable, and so in life we develop ways of adequate protection. Some retreat within their shells, others hide behind their masks, and others put on armour as a way to face the world. These veils of protection are very thin, and I am glad when I can see right through them. Without the armour or the mask and shell, conversations can be deep and real. Yet it is often hard for people to find this place, to be authentic, and so exposed, without the need to hide behind a story. Some people will never go there, not even in private. They will never enter the looking glass to explore the mystery of who they really are. So this is where we are going in this story.

In the Welsh language 'glas' is a colour. Now it means the colour blue, and once it was suggestive of the ocean and the sky. When the ancients looked above and below, they perceived themselves in the middle, above the 'glas' of ocean, and beneath the 'glas' of sky. Beyond the 'glas' there were other realms, hidden dimensions, or other worlds.

In the English language "glass" is a hard transparent substance, a window through which we look, an ideal metaphor for the glazing of perception, and a suitable place to start a journey into the theatre of soul.

So let us enter the story scene by scene – through the looking glass.

SCENE ONE **WATER** BLUE RUNE

**Keywords for WATER
and the Blue Rune**

WATER
Flow
In the flow of life
Life's Journey
Your roots
Memory
Intuition
Surrendering
Acceptance
Listening
Journey
Pilgrim, Pupil
Life-force
Lifetime
Rhythm, Music
Cash flow, Currency
Depths, Darkness
Calmness, Anxiety
Fear, Courage
Faith, Trust
Ease
Time
Taking your time
Time to rest
Feeling drained
Missing the boat
Life passing you by
Hard work, Working too hard
Overcoming obstacles and diffi-
culties
Navigating life's ebbs and flows
Letting things run their course
Ebb and flow of emotions
Sadness – Feeling blue
Moving against the current
Leap of faith, Taking risks
Caution, Foolhardiness
Going with the flow
Your Career
Your Will

The place of WATER "FLOW" The BLUE RUNE

The Blue Rune takes you to WATER, the place of flow within your home. Here you may tap into Water's energy, the carrier of your life-force, the river of your life's journey. Here you are the navigator of your own life story.

Your highest potential calls you to surrender to the flow and find courage to accept the things you cannot change, to overcome the fears that hold you back and to take a leap of faith.

In this place you will find currency and currents. Your main currency is energy or life-force, and here you make decisions about the management of your life-force, about how much you receive and how much you expend. You also choose how to spend your lifetime. Here there is all the time in the world.

This place of WATER is your energy bank account. You come here to discover how good your investments are and how much your expenditure is. When you spend your time racing against the clock, you will feel your life-force depleting. Times of rest and play and being in the moment, replenish your life-force.

Here you can feel life's pulse, you can make decisions about the currents, about those you want to move against and those you want to go with, accepting that there are moments when undercurrents you cannot anticipate will change the course of your life.

For your life to be healthy, its elements must flow. This is the place to reflect upon all things that must flow in your life: emotions, spirit, memory, intuition, career and cash. The element of WATER will always take the path of least resistance and it will carry you in this way. But you must choose how to manage its flow.

When the path of least resistance is hazardous, it is faith that will get you through; fear will find another way, trying to hold you back. Fear lives behind you, it wants to hold everything back. Fear blocks flow and wants to control your life. Faith clears a more natural path.

When you go with the flow, the less you need to row and the less you need to know. There is an easy way and a hard way to achieve anything. When you are in tune with the WATER element you work only as hard as is necessary and you follow the path that is right for you.

WATER STORIES

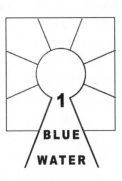

WATER is the element of 'Journey'

When I left school I was heading to be an army officer in the Royal Engineers, I did some of the training, but just could not commit to 21 years without art. Seventeen years later and fascinated by the turns that life takes, I am on a train returning from an architecture conference, now the Welsh representative of the Ecological Design Association, with one foot in architecture and the other one in homesouls. I am about to have a close encounter with the way life might have been.

WATER is the element of 'Memory and Time'

It was a long journey from Leeds back home, and by the time the train reached Wales, my carriage was empty, and I sat there alone reading my book, *"The Tao of Pooh"*. I use the book as a teaching tool, its characters are an easy way to explore the relationships between the elements: Winnie the Pooh is EARTH, Tigger is FIRE, Piglet is WATER.

A young man got on the train, he could have sat anywhere, but for some reason he came right over and sat at my table opposite me. He did not speak for a while, and then he asked about my book, and I let him know about the elemental world of Tigger, Piglet and Pooh. We chatted and joked and then I asked why he seemed so stressed. He told me he was a non-commissioned army officer and had been invited for an interview to take up a commission.

He had my attention – I had nearly taken this path, to become an Army officer. He was on his way to Swansea, because he knew someone in the record office that could show him his Army records, then he was going to Sandhurst for his interview.

I knew there was something to be learned from this man, I looked him over and then I noticed that, like me, he was not wearing a watch. I thought this most significant, as a man on his way to an interview is likely to be wearing a watch. I have an interesting relationship with watches, I have tried every type: mechanical watches, digital watches, self-winding, pocket watches, and none of them work, well not for very long. Usually they just stop and never work again, occasionally they run backwards, and sometimes they jump forwards a couple of hours.

I always pay attention when something unusual is happening with time, and this, I thought, might be one of those occasions. So I asked him why he was not wearing a watch. He said quite simply: *"I work in bomb disposal- when you are down a hole with a bomb, you don't want to see the time before you die"*.

Those were his parting words as the train pulled into Swansea station. One hour left of my journey, and I had plenty to think about. I thought about all the architects at the sustainability conference trying to build a better world, and their competition to find a good design solution to a local housing problem, and the non-architects who had put a team together in competition with the professionals.

I thought about how ironic the whole thing was, above all else it seemed to be a race against the clock, just five hours to solve the housing problem, and the big egos battled it out. I will always remember that train ride home, when memory, career, journey, all came into focus, and no one knew the time.

I got off the train close to home, and checked the station clock. It was not working. I went to the car and asked my wife Jackie for the time, she looked at the car clock and said that it had stopped, and so I crossed the road to the café, and asked them for the time, and their clock had stopped too. So we drove home through our village and passed the old station with no train tracks. We were taking our time, and the following day my little boy asked me: *"Dad, what is a long time?"*

WATER is the element of 'Going with the Flow'

Life's journey is like the flow of water, and going with the flow can sometimes mean making a difficult choice, navigating the rapids and taking a leap of faith.

A few years ago I had returned from a skiing trip with my family and we slept deeply that night, so deeply that I did not hear the water leaking. I awoke in the morning to a major flood from a burst pipe in the WATER area of my home. It had been running full bore all night.

I knew this was telling me something, and deep down I knew what it meant. I fixed the leak but I chose to ignore the message. I was enjoying my career as an architect so much and so I chose to turn a blind eye to what was calling me.

Later that day the car broke down, then two days later the wheel on the car collapsed. If this had happened at high speed on the way back from the airport we all could have been killed. I could not avoid the issue any longer and so I asked the I Ching Oracle for guidance. It confirmed what I intuitively knew: I had lost my way by returning to my career as an Architect. It said: '*If you know how to meet fate with an attitude of acceptance you are sure to find the right guidance. Danger comes because one is too ambitious. Proceed along the line of least resistance – get out of the danger. The superior man walks in lasting virtue and carries on the business of teaching.*'

I had given up teaching homesouls, lured by two commissions from homesouls clients, one to design a five star hotel on the coast, and the other to design 70 eco houses inland. This would have been the most interesting and prestigious work of my career, and so the decision finally to give up architecture was difficult, but my clients were sensitive to my homesouls work and were understanding and supportive and so it all finished amicably.

SCENE TWO **EARTH** YELLOW RUNE

Keywords for EARTH and the Yellow Rune

EARTH
Relationships
Partnership, Union
Caring, Sharing, Nourish
Bonding, Holding
Nature, Nurture
Receptive
Womb, Tomb
Your place
Body, Home, Nature
To hold and to be held
To nourish oneself
Comfort, Touching
Mothering – Smothering
Mother Earth, Goddess, Queen
Mother, Matter, Material things
Accepting the Feminine
The material world
Basic pleasures
To touch base
To be at home
Down to earth
Home comforts
Eating, feeding
Heaviness, Gravity
Worry, Depression, Over-thinking
Feeling trapped or stuck in a rut
Taking care – Paying attention
Carrying – Bearing a load
Looking after things
Labour, Working
Giving birth
Grounding
Walking

The place of EARTH "RELATING" The YELLOW RUNE

The Yellow Rune takes you to the place of EARTH within your home.

EARTH is the mother of all the elements, receiving you into her arms and holding you whilst you develop relationships with people, places and things.

It is the place of bonding, where your spirit makes itself at home amongst the material things in life, and you develop a sense of belonging. This is your home base, the place where you care for your life as a whole and surround yourself with material pleasures. In this place you want to share your life and pleasures with others, you want to nourish their needs and you want them to care for you.

Here you develop your relationship with your life as a whole, taking care of your body, home and Earth, and you experience how these sacred companions take care of you.

Your feet are firmly on the ground and you are open to receive. You savour all the fruits of the Earth, enjoying your food and your thoughts, loving to touch and to be touched, delighting in the comforts of your own existence.

This is the most feminine place of the plan, relating to the feminine aspects of your life and yourself, and female influences in your life.

This place can be your womb or your tomb. When life seems a heavy load to bear, you feel bogged down, and your cup seems half-empty instead of half-full, then your mind begins to burden you with heavy thoughts. Becoming trapped within your own life story this place can seem like a tomb with no way out. Then you may turn to the sweet taste of food and other passive pleasures for comfort.

When heaviness descends it is hard to be open to receive the calling of your Soul. The Soul will always guide you towards greener pastures: it knows the places and the people with whom it can belong.

In this place you are called to accept sovereignty over the landscape of your life. Life is your present and all the earthly pleasures are here to be enjoyed. When your life is truly nourished your cup overflows, benefiting all the people and places who share your journey.

EARTH STORIES

EARTH is the element of 'Relationships'

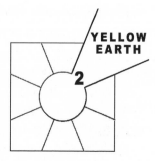

The biggest issue of the EARTH area must be relationships. Perhaps it is the biggest issue of the human condition, and I have just been told a wonderful love story about this area.

A mother, daughter and two grandchildren lived together in a small farmhouse. The mother is my friend, her daughter, who was a single parent, longed for a loving relationship, but she was a home bird, she hardly ever went out, and so she did not meet anyone, and this went on for years.

My friend did a short course with me and was inspired to go home and work with her daughter on the EARTH area of their house, which they called 'Relationships'. They cleaned the area and cleared the table, and each day on the table they lit three candles as a prayer for romance to enter the daughter's life.

On the daughter's birthday the mother placed two cards within an envelope for her. The first was a birthday card, and the second was a card of two lovers in a passionate embrace, to which the mother wrote "An invitation for love". Within just a few weeks, something amazing happened, someone special was on the scene, someone she did not have to go out to meet – he was her postman. They fell in love, and now she is expecting a baby.

EARTH is the element of 'The Open Hand'

Sometimes we have to look more deeply, beyond the subject of our desire. Some time ago, I visited a woman overseas who was very unhappy with her life. She had big plans to make things better, but she did not have the energy to achieve them. She had many issues, not all of them in the area of EARTH, but I think it is fair to say that underlying her unhappiness was the lack of a loving relationship.

It was a difficult consultation because she was not as open as I would have liked, I had to work quite hard to draw her out, and even then there were things I knew she would not tell me. To break the ice, I asked to look at her sitting room.

This was the area of WIND, and I knew it would relate to the big plans she had. We entered the room and she stood with her back to the sofa. I stood in the centre of the room, and looked around for something to catch my attention, but nothing caught my eye. Instead I sensed that there was something behind the sofa. I asked her if I could take a look, and then as if in confession, she told me what was there, and how she was embarrassed that I should find it. There was no need for her embarrassment, I was not there to judge, but to help her read her situation, and clearly I had uncovered something hidden within her story.

We pulled the sofa out to view the subject of her story. It was a beautifully carved elephant's tusk, a real tusk, the acquisition of which is now illegal. She told me in her confessional that it was a gift to her a long time ago and that she did not know by what means it had been acquired. She found the object beautiful, but was troubled by its story. I told her that we could transform her situation by celebrating the life of the elephant, and considering it to be her ally, that the presence of the tusk could be transformed to bring healing instead of guilt.

She really liked this idea, so we made a special place for it in the HEAVEN area of her home. I thought that this would help to work on judgmental issues that were so strong in her story, and perhaps its medicine would help a relationship to flourish in her life. When I spoke to her two weeks later, she had nothing to report on her relationships, and nothing to say about feelings of guilt, but she was really excited about what had happened with her health. Unknown to me she had a problem with her spleen, (an issue we did not discuss at the consultation as she did not think that working with her home could help in this area of her life.).

She had been down the orthodox route towards health, and she had been to several therapists for healing and she was having regular shiatsu treatments, which work on the acupuncture points relating to organs and the oriental five elements, but none of these were proving successful for her spleen problem. Just after my visit she went for her regular shiatsu session, and to her amazement the therapist asked what she had done because there no longer seemed to be a problem with her spleen.

She was convinced that honouring the elephant tusk in her HEAVEN area had brought the healing she needed.

I include this here as an EARTH story, because the spleen relates to the EARTH element. It is true she was having problems with relationships, but those were at the surface, there were much deeper issues, and working with the elephant tusk brought a healing touch to her story.

EARTH is the element of the 'body and the home'

The hidden landscape of the eight elements also relates to our physiology. Although I have mentioned some connections, there is so much more to say, so this may become the subject for another book, or at least a point of exploration for you to do your own research.

In tracking the correlations between the body and the home I have relied upon my wife Jackie's expertise in shiatsu, and her knowledge of Chinese medicine. Many of our clients see both of us, and the problems with their health so often correlate with a problem in their home. On the courses we teach together, our students work on both the body and the home, seeing both as a reflection of what is happening in their story.

EARTH is not only the ground that we walk upon but also the body that we inhabit and the place that we live in. Body and home are vessels that comfort, nourish and hold us on our journey through life.

SCENE THREE **THUNDER** GREEN RUNE

Keywords for THUNDER and the Green Rune

THUNDER
Awakening
Enthusiasm
Shocks, Shocking
Stirring energy
Empowering
The family tree
What you pass on
To know oneself as an authority
To know one's place within the community
Ancestors, Elders, Teachers, Mentors
Context, Influences, Conditioning
Author of your own life story
Cast your net,
Spin your web

Hope
The hero
Get up and go

Shadows, Discontent
Authoritarian, Directness, Harshness
Resentment, Anger, Aggression
Unsettling, Tension, Frustration
Stubborn and inflexible
Forgiveness and Blessings
Cutting ties – Moving on
Releasing the burdens of false conditioning
Coming to terms with responsibility
Release from burdensome pressures
Releasing anger
Clean sweeping the past

Flexibility of body and mind
Room for yourself
Vision and foresight
Planning for the future
Managing your power

The place of THUNDER "AUTHORITY" The Green Rune

The Green Rune takes you to THUNDER, the place of authority within your home. The highest potential shining through this place is to know your own authority and have faith in your own inner guidance. So when it is time to move on, you know you must cut ties with the people, places and things that hold you back, blessing them for the part they played in your life so far. Often forgiveness must precede movement and change.

THUNDER relates to how you wield your power. This area of your home is linked to the influences and conditions that shape your life. This motive force has its place of origin in the past. It sweeps across the landscape of your life. The energy of THUNDER has an unsettling effect; change can often feel uncomfortable. Before the storm there is tension, a deep sensation of the stirring energy approaching, and after the storm there is calm. The air has been cleared and the landscape cleansed.

To wield the force of THUNDER is to manage your power. You are the author of your own life story – you create your own reality.

It is the force of THUNDER that moves you into action, carrying with it the supporting power of your ancestors, elders, family and mentors.

This force drives a highway through your life, reaching into the future. It powers the visionary sense of what is to come as we reach out to grasp the future.

It is the force of awakening, helping us to see the bigger picture and calling us to action, to seize our opportunities.

When our creative power is managed well, we recognise the authority of who we are and we respect the authority of those whose influence might benefit us. We have a sense of direction and a sense of connection with the past.

When THUNDER is stirring we can feel frustration, tension and anger. When it is channelled we feel a sense of purpose and enthusiasm, and become flexible in the body/mind.

The energy of THUNDER moves throughout our community, through every encounter we have.

We are all co-authors of our life scripts. With every meaningful encounter an aspect of life unfolds into another episode of our life story. Together we co-create our lives. Often the experience is difficult or painful. Sometimes we hold others accountable and blame them for who we are. Through forgiveness we can recharge our life-force and this helps us to move on.

THUNDER STORIES

THUNDER is the element of 'Elders, Ancestors and Mentors'

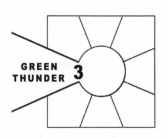

GREEN THUNDER **3**

Jackie and I were teaching in Swansea. It was a two day workshop, and we were half way through the first days teaching, the smell from the restaurant below was wafting through the big window, and the group were clearly distracted by the prospect of a good lunch. We had journeyed a long way in half a day, and our stomachs were calling. Just one more element to consider before taking our lunch and it was time to focus on THUNDER, to consider its influence in our lives.

I said, *"Thunder is the area of our elders, ancestors and mentors, of all those who stand behind us, behind the scenes".*

I paused, and in that moment the big window to my left blew out and fell to the ground outside the restaurant below. We all gasped, taking the moment in, and on that note we adjourned to take our lunch with the thoughts of what had just happened, to think about our stories in this scene.

THUNDER is the element of 'Being the author of your own life story'

We can follow our story lines to where they lead us, backwards, forwards or behind the scenes. In THUNDER the human race is like a baton race, a relay race in which we line up one behind the other: grandmother and grandfather pass the baton on to mother and father, and they in turn pass it on to us. Rarely are we conscious of what is written in the script, and yet we pass it on.

The sap that rises in us runs throughout the family tree, some repeat the same old patterns, others choose to live in a different way, but always there are influences, circumstances that condition what we believe, and the way that we behave.

THUNDER is a force within us, through which we are connected to all those in our circle, in the past, the present and the future, to the extended family and the social conditions of our society.

We can draw support from behind this scene, but we must realise that we hold the script, we are the authors of our own life stories, and we have sovereignty over life within our own castle. To find one's sovereignty, and to become the author and the authority of ones own life story is what this area of the home leads us to. When I look at life within the stories of this place, so often I uncover, resentment, shock and anger, and so much need for blessing and forgiveness, and for the guidance of a good authority.

There are so many circumstances in life, where the act of blessing and forgiveness would help to move things forward. So many suffer under the element of THUNDER, from the abuse of power that leads to entrapment, and from the over bearing authority that lowers self-esteem.

THUNDER is the element of 'Authority and Enthusiasm'

We can be hard upon ourselves, taking the outside influences in, swallowing a story line that is sometimes hard to follow.

One client said to me, "I used to be more pushy, now I seem to have lost the energy to be driven. This is one reason why I called you in – I have become stuck. Maybe I have more fear now that I have become more 'goody goody'. I don't have so much fun. I used to follow my instinct, now I just go around and around in circles. I don't seem to have the same faith that wonderful things will happen. On a bad day I think this is how it is going to be forever. I had a much better time when I was naughty and leading a more unhealthy life. I wanted to become a rock to help others, I think that is why I became a teacher, but now I am helping others and my own needs are not being met."

She has jumped into the role of 'Authority', and taking this role so seriously has given up the LAKE to build her castle in THUNDER. But her story does not suit her, and THUNDER has so much more to offer than what she is experiencing.

THUNDER is a powerhouse, it is the engine behind enthusiasm, it is the energy I call upon when I give talks and do consultations, it gets people enthusiastic, it gets things moving, and it gets things done. It is so difficult to be an enthusiastic authority if you are living a life you do not believe in, and that was her problem. We have got to get this right.

THUNDER is the element of 'Blessings and Forgiveness'
Often it is our attachment to stories and people from the past that holds us back, leaving us with things to resolve in our own minds and in a practical way, forgiving others and letting them go with our blessings, so that we can move on.

David was a gay man in his forties. He did not want me to visit his house because he said his partner would not understand, so instead he came to my office for a reading. He told me that his main issue was with his partner, and that he wanted to move to a new house without him.

With this issue in mind I asked him to take two Glass Runes from the bag. First he chose the Turquoise Rune, he put it back, gave the bag a shake and then chose another, this time it was the Clear Rune. The reading was:

Turquoise/Clear   **Lake/Unity**
Life is your present

Do not grieve for what you cannot have.
Do not grieve for what you cannot know.
Do not grieve for life that has now past:
Anoint your dead and let them go.

Make your peace with what was never said,
and with all that never was to be.

Never want to have your time again,
just say and do what must be said and done.

Let the heart rest in peace.
No regrets – Life is your present.

I have developed homesouls Oracle cards, with images that relate to the readings. David was the first client to use these cards, and this is how the consultation went:

Lindsay: *Does this make sense to you?*

David: *Yes, this is exactly what I needed to hear.*

Lindsay: *Now look at the turquoise Oracle card for this reading.*
What do you see in this picture?

David: *I see an individual embraced in the ocean of life. I love the colour turquoise of the ocean in the picture – you can see that, I am wearing a turquoise T-shirt today. I love that colour. It reminds me of Botticelli's 'Venus' rising from the sea in a shell. This is how I see myself – as a resurrecting being recreating my life. The image in that painting is like a resurrection. Do you know the painting?*

Lindsay: *Yes, I know the painting.*

David: *My grandmother appears to me regularly in dreams. She appears in turquoise, just like the image in your oracle card. Usually she is radiant, but recently she appeared to be dying. I sensed she was telling me that I am starving, not getting any nourishment from my situation.*

Lindsay: *Clearly the homesouls Oracle reading relates to the dream of your grandmother. It says: "Do not grieve - Life is your present - anoint your dead and let them go – No regrets".*

Every issue in your life has a physical place in your home. Now take just one Glass Rune from the bag, to locate where this issue lives in your home.

David: *The Green Rune – so that is the THUNDER area.*

Lindsay: *Describe the Thunder area of your house to me.*

David: *It's the hallway where the cats sleep. There is a lovely wooden stair there. Crystals, and plants are on the windowsill. There is a bracket clock on a corner shelf on the wall. The walls inside the house including the stairwell have been stripped right back to the stone. The stone is red, shot through with black and cream, with lots of quartz crystal and seashells in the rock. I really like the seashells in the rock.*

Lindsay: *Tell me about the bracket clock.*

David: *I bought it when I was shopping one day with my partner, because it reminded me of a clock my grandmother used to own. It has a shell motif carved on the front and this reminds me of my grandmother's old cabinet in her drawing room – it had a shell on it and she kept her best china in it. I can see how all this ties in: Venus, the shell, the walls, the clock the reading, and my grandmother – You are right, my story IS here in this place. I bought this clock with my partner. The shells here are so meaningful.*
I believe I have had two past lives with him, in both lives we were married, and I was the woman. In one life he was responsible for my arrest and incarceration in a prison and in another life he was an alchemist and was put to death by the officials of the church for his beliefs. Even in this life he still suffers and I feel a strong attachment and a need to protect him. Yet I also came back to him in this life to help resolve something. But that cannot happen unless he changes his ways – he is

what used to be called an unrepentant Soul.

Lindsay: *the Secret of Home is about the story of our lives. It does not matter whether the past lives you speak of are imaginary, real or true, they exist in your story, and therefore their image is etched into the place that you inhabit. You can now work with the image, to change the way things are. Do you want me to help you?*

David: *I think now I want to go home and take a fresh look at my place. I get told to do things a lot. I want to go home now and decide for myself what to do.*

Lindsay: *You are the Author of your own life story.*

SCENE FOUR **WIND** ORANGE RUNE

**Keywords for WIND and the
Orange Rune**

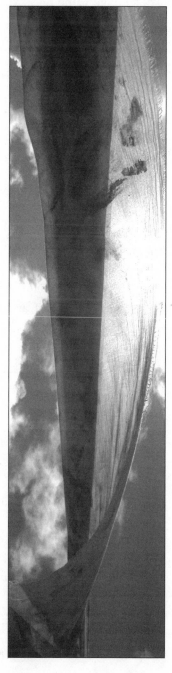

WIND
Ego
Survival
Sex drive
Competition
In search of identity
Growing up, Independence
Making your way in the world
Providence, Fortune
The winds of change
Time management
Risk management
Planning, Commitment
Focus, Ambition, Drive
Busy body, Busy mind
Rushing and racing
Frustration
Patience, Tolerance
Taking your time
Indecision, Wandering
Living in the future
Feet not touching the ground
Pioneering, Achieving, Opportunities,
Temptations, Expectations
Your honour code
Motivation
Penetration
Ideas and Visions
Breaking new ground
Commitment, Perseverance,
Endurance
Transformation, Alchemy
Movement, Growth
Flexibility

The place of WIND "DRIVE" The Orange Rune

The Orange Rune takes you to the place of WIND in your home. Here blow the winds of change in your life. Sometimes they are gentle and you have time to prepare, sometimes they come quickly and sweep you away.

WIND is your vehicle, the force that moves you through life, carrying you to people, places and things beyond where you are now, and dropping its seeds of change along the way. You can ask yourself, what is this place for me? Is it my pit stop, where life rushes by and I quickly catch a few moments for myself? Is it my control tower where I manage my time and my movements? Or is it my 'OZ', the place of the wonderful wizard, where anything can happen "in the blink of an eye"?

From here you choose how to drive your life, visualising destinations and goals and making choices about how to reach them. This is where you climb the social ladder, the career ladder, and the stairway to heaven. With ambition you push hard, without focus you simply drift, and when you go with the flow you find the way that pulls you.

Here you consider who and what pull your life strings, and from what source your motivation comes. This is where you accept your position in the human race, deciding where to place yourself and how to run your race. You decide whether to be goal or process-orientated. With too much focus on end results you miss out on life along the way. The race against the clock is a race that can never be won, because when it sets the pace, you spend your time counting time instead of living it. Life is made up of moments, not seconds, and the way to spend life-time is by living in every moment.

The winds carry many seeds, bringing many opportunities. Not all of them are for you. Here you choose what seeds to sow. If you expect to do too much in life your feet will barely touch the ground.

Here your wishes are granted and good fortune comes to you, so be careful what you ask for.

In this place of abundance the winds of change blow towards

you. They can transform your life, helping you to make new beginnings and start new journeys. You must choose how to meet the WIND.

WIND STORIES

WIND is the element of 'Pioneering, Vision and Commitment'

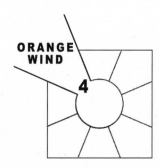

At a house warming party I was sitting with a small group of people, chatting generally, and when the conversation turned to what I do for a living, I told them briefly and they asked how I was involved with Rachel's house.

Rachel was the hostess and the woman who had built such an inspirational house. I was her architect, and hers was the only load bearing two-storey straw bale house in Britain. Rachel had called me several years before to discuss an idea she had for building a house.

Her idea at that time was not for a straw bale house, but to rebuild the old ruin, which was once the lookout for the monks of St Dogmael's Abbey. From its high perch on the hillside, it was well placed to observe the river estuary and its fertile fields.

At the party, looking out through the big windows on the site of the old ruin, the night was dark, and in the mirror of the glass, we saw only the interior and our own reflections. Interior and exterior separated only by two thin panes of glass, we were held in the space of our own reflections, a space where adventures begin, at home in the place that I call WIND.

At home in the part of the plan where dream becomes a living reality, sitting in the area of WIND, the area that holds the story of Rachel's pioneering, vision and commitment. As the story is told, perhaps it is reflecting upon the same place in our own homes, and the scenes within our own stories, where we reach out for more.

You see, Rachel had a dream that her house would be built on this site, that against all the odds, this house would be built. I tell myself Rachel's story whenever I am lacking the faith or the courage to follow a dream. I was the first person Rachel asked for help to make her dream become reality, and at our first meeting I had to be practical and professional in giving her advice, after all, I had my architect's hat on. I had to advise her that odds were definitely stacked against her. The site was remote from all public services, it could only be reached down a long narrow public footpath, and so there was no way of getting: mains electricity, mains water, public drains, or emergency services. Added to this, the ruin on the site was so dilapidated that the planning authority would normally consider it beyond repair, and its position was not suitable as a site for a new building. Rachel did not even have the money to build it, all she had was the money for my initial design.

My initial design....... Simplified for straw bale construction

WIND is the element of 'Providence'.

As is often the way when a good story is being told, interest spreads beyond the immediate circle, a few heads turn, a few more ears prick up, and in the eyes, the lights of the theatre come on. Public officials and preachers know this moment as well as story-tellers, it is the moment when the politician delivers the sound-bite, and the preacher drives home the word of God. It was the moment I had to say:

"This may be a house of straw, but its walls have substance, it is a very light house, sitting lightly on the land, taking little, and giving so much. We need light houses, and we need people like Rachel, who make a difference, pioneers with the faith and commitment to follow a dream, and

to show others that with faith and commitment, providence moves too. The house is an inspiration for any of us who lack such courage."

As I said these words (or words to this affect), as if on cue, a glass exploded into a thousand little pieces, just in the way a light bulb explodes when dropped on its end. Providence breaking glass, as if to make the point that with faith and commitment providence moves too.

Rachel was a dancer. She had no experience of building construction. She was my daughter's dance teacher, which is how I knew her. With faith in Rachel's vision, I prepared the drawings for a small house built of stone (she had not envisioned a straw bale house at that time), with living accommodation on the ground floor and a dance floor up above. She had a mountain to climb. Local residents were strongly against it, yet one by one she gained their support. But still she had the planning department to convince, and I knew from experience what she was up against. She bided her time, and when the time felt right she placed the application, then right on cue the planners appointed a new Environment Officer to look after sustainability issues.

The new appointment did not last long, but long enough for the new officer to get behind Rachel's vision – she was a dancer too. They understood each other and they had quite a lot in common, as they both had studied in the same Ballet Academy in London. Rachel got her planning permission.

The next obstacle was the Building Regulations, these govern health and safety and other technical aspects of the design. Rachel decided to become the project manager, and to my surprise the Building Regulations Department showed a keen interest in straw bale construction, and they wanted to support it. Rachel now had her work cut out, without any money, there was so much she had to do herself to research and form a good argument to support the way she wanted to build. One by one all the other obstacles fell away, and people came to help and give support.

While she was building the house, she lived in a small wooden hut with a straw bale extension. It was very peaceful there, a sanctuary for anyone who wanted to visit and share her vision.

Her father used to visit her there in the hut, and one day he said, "*Somehow the money is going to come for your house*".

Some time later, he realised he was dying, and he said happily to Rachel, "*Now you will be able to build your home*". With his money the building work began, and helpers came from all over the world to live and work with Rachel.

Now she is a dancer with a difference, she has become quite an expert in this type of construction, and a great inspiration for others who want to build this way, and to live more lightly on the land.

WIND is the element of 'Manifesting what we really want'
Fate rides the winds of change, riding with us when with faith and commitment we take the driving seat.

The WIND area of the home is to do with our abundance, growth and transformation, our aspirations and drives in life, and how well we manifest what we really want.

In one house a large piano filled the area of WIND, and on the floor there was a sculpture of a mother with a baby curled up in her arms.

I asked about the piano: "*We don't come in here, and no one plays it*," said the husband. "*It makes me feel like a child again, being compelled to play*," said the wife. "*It was a gift, but there are still conditions attached to it.*"

I translated their story into this line: *We do not play here in this area of our lives.*

So we journeyed deeper into this story, we looked at the sculpture, and we looked at practical solutions for how this area could be more integrated into their home, and how it could become a more compelling place to be. Two years later they still remember that moment of realisation. They wrote to me recently and said: "*We remember the moment as one of real enlightenment, it just made so much sense in terms of how we had been feeling and what had been happening in our lives at that time.*"

When we lack integration with this area of life, then what we wish for just does not seem to come. On the other side of the coin, life in the fast lane can also be a problem, when we drive too hard and fast we miss so much along the way, being successful is not always the blessing it appears to be.

WIND is the element of 'Good Fortune'

In the area of WIND in my home, I built a special window. Not only did it give us a great view it also brought much needed light to a dark area. At a dark time of our lives when I was struggling to make a living from homesouls, in debt and doubtful of my ability to continue with this work, the window brought us some good fortune.

The children were sitting down to eat their breakfast Cornflakes, when one of them called out, *"We could win a trip on Concorde!"* I looked at the packet, read the competition details and then turned to look at the window, saying to my wife Jackie, *"How could we win the competition when the window looks like that?"* It was a half-finished job, dismal, grey and undecorated with bare cement finishes and a temporary pane of glass.

I affirmed that if we won this flight I would take it as a sign that I was going in the right direction. So we filled the window with daffodils cleaned it up and entered the competition. Needless to say, we won! We were able to enjoy a supersonic flight and entertainment in Paris courtesy of the Cornflakes, the window and Concorde. Perhaps we would not have won the lottery for ten million that week, but this prize was enough to lift our spirits and put me back on course.

No matter how helpless or hopeless you may feel, there is always something practical you can do. Something can always be moved within your space, and with every movement you cause a ripple that finds its way into other areas of your life.

A young woman came up to me a few years ago distressed by the lack of communication with her ex- husband and with his inability to make a financial settlement. I advised her to pay attention to the WATER area of her home, to be clear about what she was asking for, then to clean the area, clear it, and place an Obsidian crystal there. The following day she phoned me to say her solicitor had just phoned with the amazing news of her husband's change of heart – that day he had signed the house over to her. Without any explanation he had made this uncharacteristically generous gesture.

Providence often needs some assistance, a sign of one's intention and a demonstration of commitment.

SCENE FIVE **UNITY** CLEAR RUNE

**Keywords for UNITY and the
Clear Rune**

UNITY

Wholeness
Balance and harmony
Whole, Holism, Holiness
Tai Chi

Tao
God
Divinity
Essence
Source

The void
Eternity, Infinity
Everything connected
All is one

Centre
To be well centred
Contentment
Home, Soul

The place of UNITY The Clear Rune

You are the scenery and the seer.

The kingdom of Heaven is in your centre.
('Gospel of Thomas', Saying 3)

Profit comes from what is there, usefulness from what is not there.
('Tao Te Ching', Ch. 11)

In the story of your life this central place is the beginning and the end, the point of departure and return, holding all that is, was, and ever will be. It is the home of belonging, the place to which longing guides you. And yet it is no place at all: without boundary, without perspective, orientation and direction, without a point of view.

To define this place conclusively is nonsense, but conceptually there is a point – you are the point.

This is the place of your Holy Grail and your paradise lost. From the void at the centre your spirit enters the wheel to animate the human race, and at the end of the race your spirit returns having completed no distance at all.

The point appeared in the circle and was not; nay, that point produced the circle.

The point in its revolution becomes a circle in the eyes of him who measured the circle.

Its beginning and end joined together when the point measured the completion of the circle.

When the circle was completed the compass put its head and feet together and rested.

We are all without Being, without Being; we are without Being and thou art Existent.

I called the whole world His dream: I looked again, and lo, His dream was himself.

From Sayid Ni Matullāh Wali in *'The Sense of Unity – The Sufi*

Tradition in Persian Architecture' by Nader Ardalan and Laleh Bakhtiar.

UNITY STORIES

So now you find yourself at the centre of the plan, in the place of number Five, the number symbolic of growth and transformation in the natural world – the first circular number.

So for continuity I have called it Scene 5, but to call it a scene is misleading, rather it is the place at the centre of the circle, the point that generates the whole picture. The infinite whole of all beginnings and all endings, it is our point of departure and return. Infinity and Unity, 'all are One', that is the story here.

So what is the point?
"The point in its revolution becomes a circle in the eyes of him who measured the circle." So said Sayid Ni matullāh Wali.

And where can I go from here?
"If the doors to perception were cleansed every thing would appear to man as it is – infinite." So said William Blake.

We enter life's story from the centre, like Alice in wonderland, down the rabbit hole, in the hall of doors. *"There were doors all round the hall, but they were all locked; and when Alice had been all the way down one side and up the other, trying every door, she walked sadly down the middle, wondering how she was ever to get out again. Suddenly she came upon a little three-legged table, all made of solid glass; there was nothing on it except a tiny golden key, and Alice's first thought was that it might belong to one of the doors of the hall; but, alas! either the locks were too large, or the key was too small, but at any rate it would not open any of them. However, on the second time round, she came upon a low curtain she had not noticed before, and behind it was a little door about fifteen inches high: she tried the little golden key in the lock, and to her great delight it fitted! Alice opened the door and found that it led into a small passage, not much larger than a rat-hole: she knelt down and looked along the passage into the loveliest garden you ever saw. How she longed to get out of that dark hall, and wander about among those beds of bright flowers and those cool fountains, but she could not even get her head though the doorway; 'and even if my head would go through,' thought poor Alice, 'it would be of very little use without my shoulders. Oh, how I wish I could shut up like a telescope! I think I could, if I only knew how to begin.' For, you see, so many out-of-the-way things had happened lately, that Alice had begun to think that very few things indeed were really impossible."*

So said Lewis Carroll.

Through which one will you enter, through number 1 to enter WATER or 2 to enter EARTH, 3 to THUNDER, 4 to WIND, 6 to HEAVEN, 7 to LAKE, 8 to MOUNTAIN, or 9 to FIRE.

Some doors will be easy, where there is no big issue with them. Other doors are harder to open when an issue is stuck, a judgement is clouded or a vision is impaired. The Glass Runes will help you choose the doors, and the homesouls Oracle readings will help you with the issues, but it is up to you to go there.

It is common to be stuck in the centre, or off at a tangent where it is hard to find the way back. The readings and the Runes will help you to navigate, so you won't stay stuck in one issue or behind one door, or even stuck in the centre, not perceiving what your options are.

We are all in the audience at the centre, the Gurus, the Mystics and the Poets too, watching our stories unfold. This is not an exclusive place, no reservation is needed; for even Gurus, Mystics and Poets have their issues out there in the wheel, we all have business out there in this theatre of Soul. In Wonderland Alice first finds herself at the middle, sadly not knowing which door to open, wondering how she is ever going to get out. In our culture we often find ourselves, separated or isolated, either stuck in the middle feeling that there is no way out, or far away from the centre of the plan.

In the modern culture of house design, the centre is often a circulation space or a less favoured area, lack of light penetrating the middle so often makes it not desirable as a place to work, rest or play. Don't be alarmed at whatever you find at the centre of your house; in so many houses I have visited there are just cupboards and storage places at the centre, often there are stairs leading to other floors, and sometimes there is a hallway full of doors. Take a look at what is there and consider your point of view. You may take the lead from Alice, For, you see, *"so many out-of-the-way things had happened lately, that Alice had begun to think that very few things indeed were really impossible."*

Being Centred - My Tai Chi Stair

At the time I built this stair it was in the centre of our small home, the place in the plan traditionally called Tai Chi. The house has since been extended and so the centre has shifted, and the stair is now an indoor garden, but we still think of it as our Tai Chi stair.

Before I built the stair there were a lot of loose ends in my life, and I wanted to become more centred. This area of the house was

originally a narrow corridor with a straight flight of stairs facing the front door. The corridor split the house in two halves, and I wanted to open it up, to give the house a sense of freedom and to establish the centre as a focal point. I had two weeks to get this all sorted while the family were away.

Unusually for me at that time I had not done any drawings, all I had was an idea for a wooden spiral stair. One hour before the builder arrived I changed my mind, I had an inspiration and I did a sketch. I knew this was meant to be and I knew we would find all the materials close by. The builder arrived and scratched his head at the drawing, he just could not figure out how to build it, so although it was not my intention, we both worked on it together. Sure enough we found all the materials close by (all within a hundred yards): slate flags (floor slabs) to make the steps, broken bricks that were intended for hardcore, and even a fallen tree that matched my drawing of the handrail.

The builder was uncharacteristically philosophical about this, saying, "this was meant to be", and then he noticed that without even realising, we had built the bottom step in the shape of a Yin Yang symbol, which is the traditional symbol for the central area of the plan.

To complete the design we built a large roof window over the stair so that houseplants would grow here, and plenty of light would penetrate the centre of the house.

SCENE SIX **HEAVEN** WHITE RUNE

Keywords for HEAVEN and the White Rune

HEAVEN
Co-operation
Attachment, Detachment
Conservation, Elimination
Helpful friends, Give and take
Boundaries, Freedom, Limitations,
Control, Censorship, Discipline
Self-discipline, Leadership
Duty, Service, Servitude
Freedom of choice
Heaven on Earth
Law and Order
Male principle
Metal
Hard, Sharp
Letting go
Sorting – Clearing
Structure – Support
Space – Placement
Breathing
Air
GOD
Utopia
Perfectionism
Idealism, Romance
Good Orderly Direction
God is in the details - The Creative
Your Calling, Destiny, Life's purpose
Religion, Dogma, Righteousness
Martyr, Servant, Good Samaritan
Community, Army, Organisation
To serve and protect, Defence
Sword, Armour, Knife
Forging links
Incisive
Less is more
The cutting edge
Technology, Information,
Networking, Communication
Logic, Intellect, Rationalism,
Skin, Barriers, Boundaries, Facades
Separation, Discrimination,
Judgement
Seeing the bigger picture,
Bounded by choices
Getting things in perspective,
Elevation, Enlightenment

The place of HEAVEN "BOUNDARIES" The White Rune

The White Rune takes you to the place of HEAVEN within your home.

Here you have freedom of choice – you choose your limitations and your response to the rational world. This place relates to your idea of a spiritual Heaven, but more than this, it relates to the way you construct your Heaven on Earth, to the choices you make about your perfect place and your perfect way of living.

It is the world as an illusion from which you shape your own reality. It is the cloth from which you cut the garment of your life, and like the emperor who made choices about his new clothes, you make choices here about what you surround yourself with: the facades you present, the barriers you put up, the boundaries you make. Here you narrow down your possibilities; through thinking and logic you discriminate and separate.

All the controls and limitations in your life are here, and in essence this is the place of your freedom. The idea of spiritual Heaven is paradise, the place where you are ultimately free. Your earthly Heaven is bounded by your choices. Here spirituality becomes religion, Love becomes romance, and judgement enters your life, shaping your circumstances and the people around you into what you want them to be.

This is the most masculine area of the plan, relating to male influences in your life and yourself.

This is the place of service and servitude. It is where we give support and receive support, it is where we connect with our whole community. It holds issues about attachment and detachment, about holding on and letting go. This is where we find the causes we want to fight for, and the missions or crusades we want to go on.

In this place we can lose sight of ourselves: we are drawn into the world outside ourselves. We network, forge links and extend our boundaries, we want to put our lives in context to understand the reasons why things happen in our lives, and to fit in. We want to make sense of it all and give our lives order.

This is the forge where you create the life you think you want and where you deal with life's challenges to that vision.

HEAVEN STORIES

HEAVEN is the element of 'The Male principle'

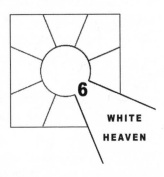

And so we move on to the area of Heaven, a place in the home that holds so many stories about the problems women have with men, and perhaps the place where men hold so many issues about themselves. This area called HEAVEN is the most yang or masculine of the plan, as the EARTH area is the most yin or feminine.

We could say that the relationship between men and women is a relationship between HEAVEN and EARTH and often caught in the middle is the child LAKE, not just the offspring of the relationship, but also the inner child of both individuals, and their creativity and self esteem.

The elements interplay, each one affecting the others. In HEAVEN, I come across so much strength, often misplaced, and sometimes the illusion of strength, where one person is forgoing their own needs to serve someone else. Here, I come across so many Rescuers, Defenders, Martyrs and strong independent people who seem to need very little help themselves, they are 'helpful friends', but no one thinks to help them, they give and do for others, but their hands are not open to receive. The open hand is an image of the Earth element; it is Yin, whereas Heaven's help is more yang.

EARTH opens to receive the force of HEAVEN, so ideas are taken in and grounded and from this creativity the things of this world are born. We breathe in and we breathe out, we take in and we let go, and in these acts of creation we enjoy the marriage of HEAVEN and EARTH, and yet, so often, things are not well within the marriage.

One woman who was brought up without her mother, said,

"Dad brought me up as a boy". Now she is very capable, not needing the help of a man. She receives so little, feeling duty bound to do so much, and in this way she depletes her energy, her life force (WATER) gets very low: machines keep breaking down, recurring electrical defects and water dripping are all outward signs of this.

Her young son does not like the sitting room, which is the HEAVEN area of their house, he does not like to go there, and he has breathing difficulties. So we worked on the HEAVEN area of her house, we looked at what was there and we made some changes. She had a large pot in that room, on one side of the pot was an image of a woman alone with a child at the edge of flowing water, on the other side of the pot was a heron and a frog. We discussed the image. The pot was empty – perhaps we should put something in it – but what? We agreed that she would place stands of willow in the pot. Willow grows on the boggy areas of my land, it is great for drawing up the stagnant water, and in this way we imagined it would draw up the stagnant issues that bog her life down.

The water in the picture seemed full of vitality, something they were both lacking. In mythology, the frog often represents sensitivity, medicine and hidden beauty, and the crane lives its life in the moment, waiting patiently in the water, for the living it represents longevity and for the dead it carries spirit into the other world.

She was clear that as the issues come to the surface, she would have to pay attention to them, and deal with them.

HEAVEN is the element of 'Control and Letting Go'

In this context, another consultation comes to mind – a house that was not allowed to breathe. All the windows were sealed closed, and the house was never aired. In this home, HEAVEN was clearly out of balance, everything was trimmed to perfection, nothing out of place, and even the garden hedge was neatly cut with a castellated top.

My advice to the woman of the house was to work in the area

of HEAVEN; this is the area that holds the story of freedom, control, limitations and boundaries. Her answer was that her husband would never allow her to alter anything in that room. It was their dining room, a showpiece, and everything had been placed purposefully by him.

Clearly they had some issues to resolve in this area – they would need to talk. She knew something about flower essences, and so instead of provoking confrontation by moving anything, she decided to spray Snowdrop essence into the room, a very subtle intervention that is used for letting go, having fun and lightening up. It would ease the flow of their conversation.

HEAVEN is the element of 'Conservation, Clutter, and Elimination'

I do not want you to think that that problems in this area always relate to excessive control, sometimes it can be quite the opposite.

One client, a man this time, had taken on many of the roles that the woman customarily assumes. He looked after the kids, did all the cooking, and he was a therapist, while his wife was more inclined towards the business side of their affairs.

One thing that characterised their house was the lack of boundaries. No one in the family seemed to have much personal space, one area spilled over into another, so it was hard to see where the kitchen finished and the sitting room started. The dining table was the wife's office, and even the sleeping areas were fairly open plan.

The place was cluttered, we all agreed about that. The husband was ambivalent towards most of the stuff, although the junk under the stairs bothered him a lot – he wasn't surprised to be told that the stairs was in the HEAVEN area, and his colon problems related to this part of the plan. In the body, the large intestine is related to the process of elimination, it sorts out the bodies waste, getting rid of what we do not need and recycling what we do need. If the waste in our lives begins to pile up, our systems have to take on extra load. He cleared out under the stairs, sorted things out and established clearer boundaries – they all felt much better.

HEAVEN is the element of 'Boundaries'

When we first moved to West Wales, 'Boundaries' were our biggest issue. Our fields were not fenced so the sheep and goats kept escaping, and the garden was not secure so we worried about our children playing so close to the road, and in the old farmhouse we had very little space, we all seemed to live on top of each other.

We entered through the back door, which opened into the centre of a long narrow kitchen. On one side of the door was the kitchen sink on the other side was the cooker, and in between was where we put our outdoor shoes and wellington boots – there was no where else to put them. To the far right of this room the HEAVEN area seemed to become a magnet for all the things that had no where else to go.

To sort it out, I decided to turn this problem into an opportunity, so I built a separating wall and converted the area into a study for my work. The effect of this was interesting, clearing this area meant more than just clearing up our physical stuff. The whole family developed a skin condition. My mother living one hundred miles away developed a very sore and congested nose and mother in law, living in America, had problems breathing. All these conditions it seemed to me related to the work I was doing in the HEAVEN area of our lives, and even our extended family seemed to be releasing toxins from the body.

In space there are no boundaries, the effect of this work was deep, it affected our family across three generations and across two continents.

SCENE SEVEN **LAKE** TURQUOISE RUNE

Keywords for LAKE and the Turquoise Rune

LAKE

Joy
Offspring
Breathing
Inspiration, Conception
Creative imagination, Ideas
Genius, Gifted
Inner sense

Return to innocence
Playfulness, Cheerfulness,
Childhood
Inner child, Eternal child
Child development
Child abuse
Freedom from Conditioning

Clown, Mask
Hiding, Something hidden
Narcissism
Self conscious
Self-esteem
Love yourself – Honour yourself

Rape and Abortion

The unknown, Magic
Dreaming, Fantasy

Sacrifice, No regrets

Seeker, Disciple, Follower
Letting go of the need to know
Nourish the root to enjoy the fruit

The place of LAKE 'INNOCENCE' The Turquoise Rune

The Turquoise Rune takes you to LAKE, the place of 'Innocence' within your home. The highest potential shining through this place is 'love for oneself'.

Creativity transcends the mundane when filled with the power of love, for beauty is the manifestation of love. Nothing in life will flourish without it, and only through love for oneself can one truly love another.

This is the centre of your self-esteem, home of your creativity, and the wellspring from which you draw the essence of who you truly are. The truth about life inhabits the invisible world beneath the LAKE. Above the surface we experience images, symbols and symptoms of the way things really are. Beneath the surface, through the depths of its reflections, lie its mysteries. This is the place where your imagination is at home and your intelligence gives way to dreaming.

Here you are the child within the adult, a being without form, vulnerable and ready to be shaped by the conditions of the world. You are completely open to life, guided by intuition, recognising the magic of every moment and seizing every opportunity for joy and play. This is the place of the unseen and the unconscious, the realm of mystery and magic where anything and everything is possible. In this place you are life's disciple, and when you bond with people, places and things you do it through love and compassion.

At the surface you are wounded and you hide what you don't want others to see. Your wounds cut deeply and you shut away the aspects of yourself that others might find uncomfortable. You put on masks and build facades to disguise how you really feel and who you really are. People will meet you at the surface, but will never get to know the deeper you. At the depth of your being is a land where only you may go.

LAKE is where your innocence and your ideas meet the world, naked and exposed, they are vulnerable and in need of guidance. This is your creative charge, a healing journey to empower your Soul. Your power lies in getting to know the invisible self beneath the surface of who you are, and honouring yourself. From this place you will direct your spirit towards people, projects and things, and in directing your spirit you direct your power. The spirit fuels the journey of life and you must manage its flow.

How will you bring your innocence and ideas into the world, what path will you take, and how will you respond to the wounds you receive?

LAKE STORIES

LAKE is the element of 'Childhood and Creativity'

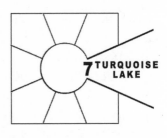

Take a look at the plan below – You will see that EARTH is top right, and HEAVEN is bottom right, between them is LAKE. Earth is Mother and Heaven is Father, Lake is Child. Earth is the Receptive, Heaven is the Creative and Lake is their Offspring. Through the marriage of Heaven and Earth many things come into existence.

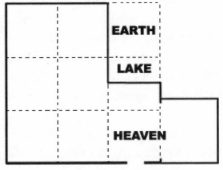

Here is a story about LAKE. In this house both EARTH and part of LAKE were missing from the plan, they were external to the house, and the couple who lived there with their child did not feel a sense of belonging. They felt there were issues for them in the house, but they wanted to move on, and that is why they called me for advice. These people were very intuitive, and I felt I did not need to travel the long distance to view their house, they could be my eyes, so we did the consultation over the telephone.

I asked the man of the house what were his key issues. He said:

Feels like something of me is missing.
I want to explore my creative side.
I want to play more.
I have been feeling I am not good enough.
I had a traumatic childhood.

I asked the woman of the house for her key issues, and she said:

At first I felt disempowered through being a mother. I did not think I was any good at it.
I questioned whether my dreams were illusions and ego trips.
I juggle focussing my creativity between being a mother and doing my work.

For this couple, we had to look at the areas of EARTH and LAKE. Issues about the role of mother are EARTH issues, those about childhood, playfulness, creativity, dreams, and self esteem are LAKE issues. These people knew that the issues in their lives were connected with their home, and that there must be a good reason why they had gone to live there, but they could not see it.

It is no coincidence that the two areas connected with their story were mostly outside not within the plan of their house; we had to look outside. So looking out through the window of their house, they described these two areas to me, looking first at a holly tree that they both loved. They said it was right on the boundary between EARTH and LAKE (mother/child), they loved to watch the blackbirds eating the berries from the tree. To them the house seemed so old and tired, but the holly tree seemed full of life and energy. This was clearly a female tree, because only the female flower changes into the holly berry. And it was clear that in relation to the mother issues, the focus of this story should be on the holly tree. They found nothing else to focus on in the area of EARTH, and in LAKE all that caught their attention was a sandpit.

We discussed the issues in the area of LAKE and I asked the man to imagine a fictitious structure that might be there. He imagined a tall structure, like a castle, rising out of an island in the Lake, so I left him with this suggestion: find a storyline in this image – be playful with your storyline, use your imagination, and build something along this line. Use the sand. Explore the area of LAKE as if you were a child, have fun with it, relate to it as if it is a part of you that you have lost – the part of you that you are looking for.

Two weeks later he wrote to me, and this is what he said:

"I thought I would give you some feedback on things since the reading. I made my castle in 'Lake'. I also drew a mother & child and hung it from the Holly Tree and filled the bird feeder in the tree, which is adjacent to the drawing that I placed. It felt like the tree (Mother Energy) was not only nourishing the abandoned child but also nature in the form of the birds. I felt a lot clearer and more at peace with my Mother abandonment issue. I'm very excited about this, as I feel I have broken free of a very old program that my body has been holding for 45 years. At last, it is so freeing. It feels like I've reached and worked through the reason for living in this house."

And so they moved on to another house.

SCENE EIGHT **MOUNTAIN** PURPLE RUNE

**Keywords for MOUNTAIN and the
Purple Rune**

MOUNTAIN
Sanctuary
Be here now
Know thyself
Original innocence
Bedrock, Touchstone, Core
The core of who you are
The rock you build your life upon
Pause, Gateway, Foundations
The threshold between inner and
outer space
The inner laws of one's being
Your sacred contract
Hermit, Prophet
Self-development
In-tuition, Guiding Wisdom
Enjoy the view – See and be seen
Set an example by taking care of
yourself
Drawing upon inner strength and
wisdom
Having patience and paying attention
Inner composure, Tranquillity
Stillness, Constancy, Stability
Keeping your own counsel
At home within oneself
Kind and gentle
Yield and overcome
Sensitive, Vulnerable
Modest, Arrogant
Stubborn and immovable
Inertia and indifference
Easy-going
Manipulative
Mindfulness, Over-thinking
Dedication, Devotion
Heaviness, Gravity
Self-contained, Aloof
Independence, Isolation
Influence through Humility
Well-grounded, Centred
Quiet mind, Peaceful heart

The place of MOUNTAIN "STABILITY" The Purple Rune

The Purple Rune takes you to the place of MOUNTAIN within your home. This is the rock at the foundation of your life, the core of who you are. It is the stillness at your centre, the home of your inner strength, permanent and unbreakable. No one else has access to this part of who you are. When you become the MOUNTAIN and your life is guided from this inner place you will always be safe. When you lose touch with your MOUNTAIN you lose your centre and become vulnerable and over-sensitive, open to others to mould and shape what you do and how you are.

The MOUNTAIN is receptive and yielding to all life's elements, but it never changes its essential nature. This place helps you to discover who you are; it helps you to realise your individuality and your identity, and to develop your relationship with self as the foundation for relationships with others. When you are at peace with yourself you are happy and well grounded in your own company. When your heart is at peace and your mind is quiet this aspect of your nature is in balance. When your thoughts go beyond their immediate situation, your heart becomes sore.

At the heart of this place everything just is. It is about being, not doing, and about seeing things the way they are. When you look upon life from the MOUNTAIN, you see your stories with clear vision; you know their illusions.

Stubbornness and immobility are on the shadow side of the MOUNTAIN. There one cannot see clearly, and independence hardens into isolation. There is no comfort in not being seen.

Looking from the MOUNTAIN you can see clearly, and when you are on the MOUNTAIN others look up to you. This is where you have the greatest influence in the world.

The greatest gift you can give to the world is to be who you truly are.

MOUNTAIN STORIES

Now we come to MOUNTAIN in the
house. This is the time to pause, to be
centered within oneself and then to take a
wider view.

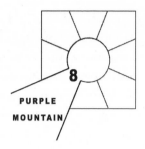

From the top of a mountain we can gain
the widest perspective.

Within the home the MOUNTAIN from which we look is the
core of who we are, it is our inner strength, the foundation on
which we build our lives.

When we look outside, what do we see? Where do we place
ourselves within the picture? How tied up in the story have we
become?

MOUNTAIN is the element of 'Modesty, Strength and Devotion'.

In casting my mind back over consultations, I realized that there is
not much drama in my MOUNTAIN stories, most of the drama
comes from the influence of other elements. So here is one such
story.

The first thing I remember was the approach to the house, it
was almost hidden from the road, through a casual opening at the
edge of the woods, then a steep ascent into the woodland, where I
had to park the car. Climbing further up the hill on foot, I reached
another clearing where a small house was built. There I met a very
small man chopping wood. There was nothing imposing about his
stature or disposition, he said very little to me, just a slight gesture
of acknowledgement. His partner; the woman I had come to see,
came out of the house to greet me, and the small man took her
daughter off for a few hours to give us some space.

Usually when I enter a house for a consultation I have a very
strong sense of where to look, and when I look I always find
something significant. This time I was most struck by the quality of
presence of the man. It felt like I was in the presence of a King, not
that I have ever been in a king's presence, and not that I mean a

normal king. I mean that there was a sense of dignity, strength and grace about this man that felt very Kingly, and this was a very strange feeling, considering his demeanour. Not only was he very short and slightly built, but he was also scruffy, and obviously did not care much for the way he appeared to be; his voice was small and his words were very few, and so I was fascinated by the way his presence had touched me.

I went into the house and did the consultation with the woman. This is not to be the subject of my story; her story was far too painful. Suffice for me to say that her life had been full of drama, none of which, as far as I was told, would be the kind of drama that we would want in our lives. She did not want it in her life either. Her issues were in FIRE and LAKE, and we found the reflections of her story there.

I want to tell you about the man in her life, because he was exactly what this woman needed. I asked her about him, and so what I have to tell you is what she told me. I still think of this man sometimes, and when I think of him I call him 'King'. So this MOUNTAIN story is about the character of 'King'.

King was always there for her; she needed his shoulder to cry on. Because of her experiences, she admitted that she was a very difficult woman to live with. She projected so much of her stuff onto him, and often she did not appreciate him. When she lashed out, he would hold her gently, when she screamed he would listen softly. He never pushed her or expected her to change. He was always there for her; her rock and her touchstone. In the strength he had, there was so much dignity, he did not suffer because of her, he did not enter into her story, he was just there for her, holding the space, because someone had to, and he asked for nothing in return.

The I Ching says, *to rule truly is to serve*. We need more people to be this strong; people who are willing to climb this MOUNTAIN. It is not just women who need this, we all suffer in the hidden landscape because the King is wounded.

In the quest to find oneself, we have to scale the MOUNTAIN. We need space, freedom, and independence to discover our own answers and to gain insights that can lead us to our own truth.

People who are strong in MOUNTAIN qualities make useful guides and touchstones.

I have a friend who is such a guide. Whenever he speaks, I listen, he does not have much to say, but whatever he does say is well considered. He used to work as a counsellor in a big institution, but his work was not appreciated, his counselling room was in a basement without windows, and where nobody could find him, which is not a good place for a Mountain man, so he could not stick it.

I am telling you about 'King' and the 'Mountain man' because they both have qualities that we need sometimes in our lives. When we can find these qualities in ourselves, we are fortunate, and our journeys are not so hard.

A character like 'King' is very centred in himself, self-contained, and not too tied up in his own story, he is a rock that one can lean on. If you possess this quality within yourself then you know how to be with the way you are, the core of you is strong. The Mountain man is a rock of wisdom; he is there if you choose to find him, he does not blow his trumpet in your ear. He is contemplative and will say things that are thought provoking.

It is wonderful to have these characters in our lives, we need them now and again when we are struggling on our journeys, and we need to find them in ourselves.

In fairytales and myths these characters often crop up. They sit at the edge of the woods, and at the foot of the mountain, we meet them when we need some strength or guidance, they help to show us a clear way through the woods, they strengthen our resolve to climb.

By describing the Mountain man and the King in this way I have made them mythical characters, larger than life, and that is all right. I am, after all, telling you a story. I can also tell you that they struggle with the same issues that we all have. I phoned my friend the 'Mountain Man' today to ask if I could include him in this story, and asked if there was anything relevant to him that I could say. He said that he keeps hearing a song by Rodgers and

Hammerstein, going over and over in his head, the words are, *"Climb every mountain, ford every stream. Follow every rainbow, until you find your dream"*. Just like so many of us he is still looking, making good progress, but not quite getting there. He is in a different place now, a different place than where I first knew him. Then he lived in the woods, remote to all but his friends. He spent a lot of time by himself, in nature and in the garden. But he was often unhappy, he had moved three times in as many years, and each place he moved to was small and remote, set in nature, but always there was something missing.

My wife and he are good friends, and she visited him a few times in his old place. The first time she was there she noticed roses stencilled on the wall, and the next time she noticed that he had stencilled some more roses. Roses to most women, are a sign of love and romance, I am told. They never talked about this, but soon after he had stencilled the roses he started to see someone, a romance blossomed and they fell in love, then he moved to a different place with her. It was called Hill House. He left the woods and climbed the hill with her, and it was not long before they got married.

In his wedding speech he said, "I always admire her energy". She has so much stamina. He entered her busy life. Now life for him has changed. They run a successful business together and they both are very busy.

He said to me, *"I feel that I have to stay really anchored to keep everyone supported, staying centred, and as grounded as possible, without kind of losing myself in it all."* He said of his house, *"I don't know where the Mountain area is now, the house has a more complicated plan since we extended it."* I took this as an invitation from my friend to play my part, to be the guide who can help him find the MOUNTAIN in his house. I think it is really important for him, as it is for all of us, to be in touch with the MOUNTAIN.

SCENE NINE **FIRE** RED RUNE

Keywords for FIRE and the Red Rune

FIRE
Light
Colour
Clarity
Radiance
Expansion
Truth, Love
War and Peace
Fun, Celebration
Passion, Compassion
Image, Self-expression
Make-up, Face-paint, War-paint
Charisma, Charm
Vanity, Grace

The Heart, the Hearth
Warmth, Heat, Power
Generating, Consuming
Chaos, Rage

Spirit – Your spark
Following your light
Sensuality, Spirituality

Climax, Orgasm
Completion

Realisation, a wake-up call
Desire
Recognition
Being seen and heard
In the spotlight, Centre stage
Letting your Inner Light shine
The truth will set you free
Being true to your word
Being authentic

Beauty is the manifestation of love
Let there be light

The place of FIRE "RADIANCE" The Red Rune

The Red Rune takes you to the place of FIRE within your home. FIRE illuminates life's path, welcoming you to life's party. Here you are magnificent, radiant and luminous. You are in life's spotlight and all that is good and true about you shines through. Your light reaches out to touch others and they can feel your warmth. Here your life is filled with grace.

When you are true to yourself and filled with love the FIRE in this place burns brightly. FIRE is the spark that ignites your life, it burns most brightly when filled with spirit and joy, and when you are in love with your life.

When love of life and truth are missing, FIRE will look for artificial fuel, then its desires become unquenchable, and the life it nourishes becomes shallow and vain, turning to consuming, possessing, and making false impressions. FIRE without good fuel becomes dim and darkness enters, there is little clarity and it is hard to find the way.

In the warmth of FIRE you will find peace, in the flames of FIRE you will find passion, and in its reflections compassion. In the light of FIRE there is no place to hide, people recognise you for who you are, and you shine as an example for others to follow.

FIRE is the power that lights the flower; its beauty is the manifestation of love, stirring in us the desire to live life to the full, filling us with passion, and helping us to see more clearly.

FIRE is the power invested in your spirit, so make empowering choices that reflect who you truly are. Channel your energy only into things you believe in, speak your truth and follow it through.

FIRE STORIES

FIRE is the element of 'Passion'

In one couple's bedroom I could sense there was a problem with passion, but they were not going to confide in me that much, so I spoke hypothetically, talking of a hypothetical person, the affect of the colour

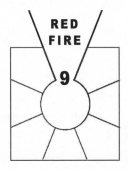

RED
FIRE

9

red, and the sexual image of an amaryllis flower. I knew they had taken all of this in, and the little they did divulge was that they had been trying for a child and had been unsuccessful. I saw them again about 11 months later, they came over for a chat at a health show, their baby in a pushchair was about two months old, and had been conceived shortly after my visit.

FIRE is the element of 'Love'

A single woman I visited was about to make a commitment to her partner, for them to live together and to share their lives. The morning I visited her she had just been told she was pregnant.

Independence had been a big issue in her life, and whilst she loved her partner she had reservations about how well they would live together. This was a core issue in her life, so I wanted to look at the central area of her home, UNITY.

What I found was beautifully revealing. They had knocked two fires into one to make an open fire. I asked about the fire, and she said they had not tried it; the chimney sweep had said that because it still had two chimney flues it would not work as one fire. So the issue here was reflected in the image of this Fire: two flues for one fire.

FIRE is the element of 'Completion'.

This is about a couple who were finding it hard to sell their house. They felt that they were stuck with the house, it seemed to them as if it were holding them. It seemed to me that there were unresolved issues that still held them there, and that until they had some completion in their relationship with the house, the house would not be seen in its true light by potential purchasers.

In my earlier story about Laurence and Jayne, the desire to move was held back by THUNDER. Anger with what had happened in the past was still present in their lives, resolution and forgiveness was needed before they could move on, and they needed to take more time. In this more recent consultation, the issues are clearly different, and since my time with Laurence and Jayne, I have developed the working technique, so now clients can do their own readings from this book.

I offer the bag of Glass Runes, with an instruction to focus on a question, and then to feel around in the bag and pick out the Glass Rune that feels right. The question asked here was *"why can't we sell our house?"* The first Rune was chosen (Red), then put back in the bag, and then a second Rune taken in the same way (Purple). Red/Purple is FIRE/MOUNTAIN. The reading is called "Longing".

You can turn to the full reading in Chapter 4.

This is a summary:

Red/Purple FIRE/MOUNTAIN "Longing"

Mountain is our inner home. Fire is the light that guides the way through the inner and outer landscapes of our lives.

These runes call you to know that longing is a heartfelt calling of the Soul to find your way back home…When you feel you don't fit in or you lack direction, feel ungrounded and discontent, you have lost your connection with your inner home…When you judge yourself and others, you build a prison deep inside.

Learn to have a lighter touch – the ability to touch people's lives and then move on, to be centered in your approach, gentle, modest, adaptable and cheerful, knowing how to meet changing situations, secure in your belonging, at home within yourself. A fire on the mountain is a temporary pleasure: like a travelling minstrel it brings light relief and then it is gone. Those who are arrogant, aloof or guarded cannot touch the hearts of others.

FIRE is the element of 'Truth and Clarity'

Their longing is to sell the external home, but the issue lies with the inner home; in their relationship with themselves, and in touching the hearts of others. We decided to look deeper, and so asked this deeper question: *"What is the calling of my home?"* This is a primary question, at the foundation of every issue within the house. It means, *for what reason has destiny, fate, and my choices, guided me to this place?*

The answer is given as if in a lesson: that this is what you are here to learn. (I still consult the I Ching for the answer to this question). Here the answer was hexagram 42, WIND/THUNDER, and Confucius statement is most interesting: *"The superior man sets his person at rest before he moves; he composes his mind before he speaks; he makes his relations firm before he asks for something..."*

I suggested they sat down with pen and paper and asked themselves the following questions:

- What have you learned whilst living here?
- What have you gained whilst living here?
- How have you helped others?
- What burdens have you released here?
- What extra burdens have you come to bear here?

We discussed the need to recognize that good will come even from the problems associated with their place. I asked them to write down what actions they could take to address the issues above, and then to take action that would touch the hearts of others.

They told me that they had done a lot of Soul searching whilst living here, and so the reading made sense to them. They thought it a good idea to gather their thoughts on what had happened as a closing chapter to their story there. Living there, they were now feeling listless and stuck, and no one was coming to see the house.

We asked, *What main area of the house should we work on in order to sell the house?*

Taking just one Glass Rune from the bag this time, the selection was the Red Rune, so the answer was in the FIRE area of the house.

In their house the FIRE area was designed to be the entrance, but it was not used as the main entrance. They went around to the back door, and entered the house through the Utility Room, and visitors also came to the back door.

We looked at ways of directing potential buyers to the more impressive front door in the FIRE area, and we looked at the potential for making the house more attractive to a buyer. FIRE is the element of clarity and light. We looked at interior design, colour, clearing it out and lightening it up. I suggested placing fresh flowers in the entrance and improving the lighting there, lighting candles in the FIRE area as an invocation for their house to be seen, and for someone to like it enough to buy it.

FIRE is like a spotlight illuminating the stage. When we focus on FIRE we take center stage, we enter the spotlight. We know we are in FIRE when we are focussing on how things appear to be, on how the place looks and what other people might think. When we are selling a house this is important, but the spotlight shines much deeper, it penetrates the scene, entering the inner beauty of the story.

My clients often want something in particular; to sell their house, to find love, to gain more recognition, to have more passion, and often these things will come, but sometimes at a price.

FIRE brings clarity and with this clarity 'truth' shines through, sometimes exposing more than they had bargained for.

Chapter 3

Reading your home

My daughter Charlottes first drawing of a house, age 7

Reading your home

Your home is a mirror of yourself
It tells the story of your life
Is a living Oracle
A dream catcher
And a vessel for life's journey.

It calls to you and you can call back.

Reading your home will help you to become the architect and the author of your own life story, working with the space that supports your everyday life to make yourself at home within the context of your story.

Homesouls attracts people for many reasons. Some are at a crossroads or a crisis point in their lives, wanting to change direction or put things right. Some want to create more harmony around them or to be more spiritually aware of their living environment. Others, like me, are really fascinated by the way our lives are so intimately connected with our homes.

In the popular culture of Feng Shui so many people are now looking to their homes for the cause of their problems. This is because some influential Feng Shui teachers encourage us to believe that problems in our homes create problems in our lives.

I would like you to take a far more optimistic view, seeing the problems within your home as reflections of much wider conditions in your life. In my view all the issues in our lives are reflected in the details of our homes.

The first step on the homesouls journey is to uncover the issues that live within your home and to recognize the details that are calling for your attention.

Your home is a vessel, providing nourishment and supporting you on life's journey. Like a nest, it holds you while you grow. It holds your whole life story and helps you to go with its flow. Homesouls is a way to work with your life script through the interior of your home.

People often ask me: *So what is wrong with my home?* or *What is causing this problem in my life?* They fear that something is out of place or attacking them. But nothing is out of place. Everything simply reflects the way things are. It is a shame when fear overrides our more positive emotions. Hope has more generative power.

We are not all equipped to be therapists, physicians and psychologists, but we can all nourish the space in which we live. If you tracked the energy of a problem, I believe you would find its root to be not physical but spatial. Every possibility exists in the space we inhabit. Beyond the boundaries of what we see, feel and think we are called to make contact with the numinous space of wholeness and unity connecting every person, place and thing. So we can call to this space for help and healing, and from the numinous, what we need will come.

The humble act of cleaning the home and lighting a candle is like a prayer, there is power in it. All our acts of creation are homoeopathic, and the good intentions behind them draw nourishment from our spaciousness. We are all physicians of our own personal space. The body is our first skin, identity/image is our second skin, and the home is our third skin.

It is creative and empowering to view a problem within the home as symptomatic or symbolic of a much deeper condition. This attitude to Feng Shui is compatible with the general approach in holistic medicine. If, for instance, you went to the homoeopath showing outward signs of stress, she would be likely to delve deeper into your circumstances to determine how this life condition has manifested in your physical body. She would try to discover a more complete story, and her cure would be based upon this. The homoeopathic tablet is not actually the cure. Through the tablet a specific message is conveyed to your in-built healing mechanisms. It is as if within the tablet there is some sort of memory which the body needs in order to regulate itself. In fact, the active ingredient within the homoeopathic tablet is so minute that only sophisticated equipment can measure it, and in the most potent tablets there is hardly a physical trace of the active ingredient. So when the homoeopath has found your problem, she has found the opportunity to make things better for you. She doesn't heal you, she helps your body to heal itself with the aid of a tablet containing the correct message for the job. It is the same principle with flower remedies, aromatherapy, and healing through touch, and it is the same with homesouls.

This approach is a journey, an exploration to find the hidden messages within the details and the story of your home – a quest to find what is missing or out of balance in your life and to become more centered in your story and in your living environment. Success with homesouls does not require an expert to visit your home, although there is much to be gained from another's deeper knowledge and wider experience. It is a process for self-discovery.

Look at your home to reveal its story; don't be surprised to find that the parts of your home you like the best relate to the aspects of your life you enjoy the most, and your problem areas relate to the more difficult qualities of your life.

In Feng Shui there are so many ways and so many contradictions in theory and practice, yet all the different methods seem to be successful. How can this be?

The common thread is people entering into a positive process and engaging deeply with their living environments. Their intentions and their creative actions are instrumental in bringing about the desired changes. The space they work in and the objects or qualities they bring to the space help in the process, but the things in themselves are not the cures, they simply carry the message.

Scepticism or the desire to know exactly how it works only gets in the way, inhibiting intuition and blocking the flow. Of course, it is healthy to have an enquiring mind, but being too literal does not help the homesouls process. If you can allow your intuition and imagination to guide you, then discovering the Secret of your Home will be a wonderful journey.

We are navigators and authors of our own life stories. We must call for change creatively – creativity is the language of change, so we must focus our creativity to make changes that are appropriate. Creativity is a spiritual lifeline, pounding through the heart deep down to the Source to bring truth, love and beauty into this world.

Everything in our lives has a context. We place everything somewhere, we literally give our things a home and we make ourselves at home somewhere. We place ourselves and others within the context of our stories, and we imagine where we might be in the future and remember where we have been in the past. Even if thoughts, feelings and belongings do not have a physical place, they do have a place within the memory and imagination. Place is different from space. Space is without boundary and without tangible presence. All the aspects of our lives that cannot be measured or defined inhabit our space: the ambience of a room, the love we have for someone, the unconscious, our life-force energy, Spirit, Soul and Divinity, these all exist in space. Beyond what we perceive through our five senses and beyond the physical boundaries in which we are present, we exist in space. The "Space" I am talking of is "Soul".

We place ourselves in the world. Our sense of place grounds us, it is earthy, gives us a physical home and a physical presence. Place is like the surface of a mirror – we define ourselves and our lives by what appears to be there, but beyond the mirror there is simply space.

The physical world is the symbol and image of the spiritual world. Whatever we perceive in our place exists in space. We cannot perceive things in space; the mind needs a context in which to place things in order to understand them.

Our memories, experiences, concepts and ideas give our lives its context, and we build our walls around these – the way we see our lives becomes the way we inhabit our lives.

Home is like a looking glass through which we can see our life stories, but we need to look beyond what we see, beyond the surface reflections of our lives and into the space where love, memory, life force and divinity exist. Home is a vessel in which we journey through life, within its walls we can open doors to an invisible landscape to take a closer look at our lives and close the gap between pleasure and pain, longing and belonging.

I am sure that we all enjoy life most when things are going well, running smoothly and everyone is happy. Yet this is not the way it goes for most of us, all of the time. Sometimes there are trials of life, and through these trials, when things are changing, not going to plan, or falling apart, we begin to question and reassess.

I have never been called to a house to look at how well things are going. That is not the point. Home serves like a mirror reflecting images of the way to Soul. The way to Soul is through what does not quite fit: Something is out of place, disjointed, not working, troublesome, or simply calling for attention.

A musical friend
A friend of mine moved house, and I helped her to move into the new place. Well, I helped her to move most of her things in, one thing would not fit. The thing that would not fit was most interesting and most relevant to this new move in her life. You see, her old business had recently folded and she longed to be a professional singer-songwriter, but to pay the new mortgage she had taken a job that wasn't so fulfilling. Interestingly, it was her piano that we could not get in, because the front door into the WATER area was stuck. It needed a locksmith to release it. Everything else went into the house through the garage door but the piano sat outside under polythene all night. The WATER area relates to issues about Career, Music, faith and going with the flow.

A leap of faith
On faith and commitment, I have this story to share with you. I arrived at a client's house to find it completely bare of furniture and decoration, apart from one particularly impressive fireplace. Despite having very little money, no job and a serious eating disorder, the client was convinced a visit from me would help her out. Her boyfriend questioned the sanity of spending money on me, but she told him that soon he would see that her intuition was right.

The following day he returned home to find this magnificent fireplace in her house. Amazed and concerned he asked how she had got it, and she told him: *"At the hairdressers I mentioned I was having a visit from the homesouls architect. The hairdresser said: 'Then you must be interested in interior design. Would you like to have this fireplace? We are ripping it out to do a modern refit here'."*

The boyfriend, being a practical builder, said: *"But that's worth thousands!"* To which she replied: *"It was a gift. I told you my intuition was right!"*

Boosted by this positive affirmation, she entered enthusiastically into the consultation and design process. We mainly looked at the EARTH area of her home, knowing this to be the place reflecting her eating disorder and the lack of nourishment in her life. Her kitchen, little more than a camping stove on the floor, was in the HEAVEN area of her home. We worked on plans to make a proper kitchen in the EARTH area. Our paths crossed again about six months later and she was excited to tell me that the kitchen was finished, she had a good job and her eating disorder had vastly improved. She was looking great and feeling very positive about her life, and I took this story as confirmation that once there is commitment, providence moves too.

The fairytale house

Often in our homes we may find our trail along a fairytale, because fairytales follow story lines with age-old themes, so they make our

My sketch of the clients house.

condition larger than life.

To get to my next client's house I went up a hill, made my way beneath the trees, took a left turn towards the hill of limestone, and found myself in a clearing in front of a house made of stone. 'A sanctuary!' I thought. 'A place where a Hermit might live – a man who is strong, with MOUNTAIN qualities, full of wisdom, but distant and alone in his story.' As his story unfolded it was clear that this was so.

He was a psychologist, and like the wise old hermit in so many fairytales, his role was to give guidance. He mainly helped couples with relationship problems, and paradoxically the main theme in his personal life was 'separation'. Interestingly, his favourite possession was a picture of a cave, and not surprisingly it was on the wall in the MOUNTAIN area of his home. The new love in his life had recently moved into his house, but she was finding it difficult to fit in. I spoke to her about this and the voice of his old partner came like an echo to her mind. It said: *"I always felt there was a bit of me under the stairs with the dogs."* These apparently were the old partner's parting words.

Beneath the stairs there were no dogs now, but boxes filled with his new partner's things, and on top of the boxes he had placed a doormat; a metaphor that neither of them was comfortable with. Under the stairs was where she kept her shoes, so for our theme we considered the role of shoes in fairytales, removing the doormat and discussing the design of shelving onto which she could place her shoes.

For inspiration I offered the story of Cinderella's Silver slipper, but at the back of her mind she held the more foreboding story of the Red Shoes, a story that warns of a woman's loss of passionate vitality through taking on a too tame life. You can read the Red Shoes story in *Women Who Run with the Wolves*, by Clarissa Pinkola Estes, see Book references at the end of this book.

A mythology of home

In a society so structured by rationality and logic, it is easy to disregard the relevance of mythology in our lives. In former times

around the globe, 'Mythos' was no less true than 'Logos', now rationality and logic are scouring and sanitizing our lives. How much further will we take them? How long can a person suffer the loss of magic and mystery?

In this next story the mythology of home was very close to the surface. I remember the occasion vividly. I sat down opposite my client and we talked deeply about the problems she was having in her life. I named her problems as being characteristic of WATER and HEAVEN, to which she replied: *"You will be amazed at what I have in my garden."* I was – she had recently excavated an old ceramic sink clutched by the roots of a tree. But I knew there was more, so turning to a book on trees, I found its image. It was called a 'Tree of Heaven'.

Calling home

Sometimes deeply buried issues come to the surface with surprising results. As one door closes, another door opens, and what comes through is very welcome.

This happened to a friend. His daughter had come of age and decided to leave home to make a life of her own. He was missing her and wondering about his role as a father and about what authority and guidance he could now bring to her life.

I advised him to clean up the area of THUNDER in his house and he decided to do some DIY work in that area. The work was in progress when the telephone rang. She spoke, and with baited breath he listened. The voice was not his young daughter who had just left home, but another child he had fathered many years ago, who was now a grown woman. She was a baby when he had seen her last.

Working in this THUNDER area of blessings and forgiveness had stirred things up and she had felt the need to find him and to call him. The wheels of change moved and stirred the elements in the story of these two lives.

Diana's story

'Deconstruction' is the art of Soul building, it is our personal survey, looking at life through the details of the home is one way to enter the theatre of Soul. This survey has to take place before we can rebuild, and as we undo or disassemble the image of the home, we enter the theatre of our story. Sometimes this can be as simple as removing a picture, or taking it down and moving it to a different part of the house where its image and story seem to make more sense. Sometimes the deconstruction can take more time, even many years.

I want to tell you about Diana. I have been working with her for four years. When we first met, her life was in a bit of a tangle, particularly her relationships, and she knew that sorting her house out would help, but where to start, and what to do? This was why she called me in.

Diana had been living in the house for four years, and had been working with Feng Shui for several years. She did not like the way the house worked, and she wanted to make some changes. She had some strong ideas about what to do but she was not sure whether it was worth investing her money, time, and energy in them, so she had been sitting on these ideas for quite some time. She thought I could help because not only do I work with my own particular brand of Feng Shui, but I am also an architect, and she wanted some design assistance with how to rearrange her house.

So we were about to embark on a journey around Diana's house, to look at her home as if looking at a mirror of her life. Through looking in the right way, we enter the mirror to uncover what is happening behind the scenes.

In the Arthurian tales of the quest for the Holy Grail, the journey starts with the question, *'What Ails Thee?'* In a sense, whenever we wonder, *'What ails me?'* and   *'What is wrong with my life?'* a door opens with an invitation to enter, to journey behind the scenes, and to find what would make one's life more whole.

So I start with a question that will open a door, I ask the homesouls Oracle:

'What is the Calling of Diana's home?'

This is the most important question one can ask about their home. It means, 'Why am I here?' Or 'What is the big lesson for me to learn here?' Generally there is only ever one Calling and when you have finished with the Calling in that place, it is time to move on, somewhere else will call you.

For this reading I took one Glass Rune from the bag, placed it back in the bag, gave the bag a shake and then took another. The two Runes chosen for Diana were Blue/Yellow, they represent WATER/EARTH, so the calling of her home was *'Being an anchor in the community'*. (See the full reading in Chapter 4).

So then I asked: What is the most important area of the house for Diana to work on?

Taking just one Glass Rune from the bag this time, the Rune picked was Turquoise. So the area of LAKE in her house is the most important area for her to work on, this is where she will make the most progress with the main issues in her life.

My third question was: What is the second most important area of the house for Diana to work on? The Rune picked was Purple (MOUNTAIN).

I recommend not working on more than two areas at a time. So at Diana's house I was particularly keen to question her about LAKE and MOUNTAIN issues and to take a close look at these areas of her home, particularly with regard to her Calling, "*Being an anchor in the community*".

The journey always starts with a question, so I asked Diana what was troubling her about her house. She said she had plans to rearrange her house, and she had read a lot of Feng Shui about the different areas, but she could not see how they were interconnected, and how as a whole they all relate to the bigger picture of her life. Diana is a therapist, and her clients visit her for treatment at her home. She did not like clients coming into the house, so her plan was to move the treatment room into the garage, which would give her an extra room in the house as a family room. Taking out a wall between the family room and the kitchen would make the kitchen more spacious and light, and would create a better social space for the family. The far end of the kitchen could then be turned into a study area.

Working with Feng Shui, Diana had been focussing on three areas. The area I call WIND was described as the 'Wealth' area in her books, FIRE was referred to as the 'Fame' area, and EARTH was the 'Relationships' corner, so she had been working in these three areas to try to get more money, more recognition, and a better relationship. She had been working on each area independently of each other. I wanted to broaden her horizons, to help her see that the story of her life was interwoven between all the areas, and to see her home as a treasure trove of life stories.

In the search for treasure we need to find some clues. The word 'clue' comes from the Anglo-Saxon 'clew', meaning a 'ball of thread', with the clue we pick up a line that we can follow through the house as it weaves backward and forward through the different areas of the plan. Eventually it would lead us back to the

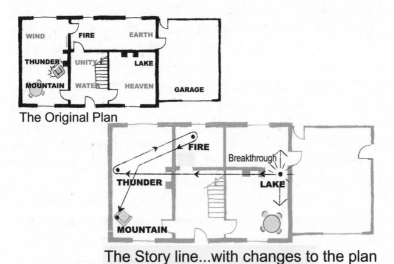

The Original Plan

The Story line...with changes to the plan

centre, to where the story first began. We navigate through this place, with nine points on the compass and nine Glass Runes in the bag in hand.

Now looking back over the past four years since my visit, Diana can see the connections between the different places in her home and the way that her story has played out in her life.

So here is Diana's story, we pick up the thread in LAKE.

The main thing Diana wanted me to look at was the idea of taking a wall down to connect two rooms in her house. The wall was in the area that I call LAKE, and this area in the plan holds our stories about childhood and self esteem. Having already done the readings for Diana's house I knew that demolishing the wall was a good idea.

So let's start with 'The Calling' of Diana's home. The reading is *'Being an anchor in the community'*.

Let me put this into context. "*Once upon a time*" Diana was called to live in this house, she did not know what the Calling was, she just knew she had to live here. This place just seemed right for her, but as time went on she was becoming disenchanted, she had followed the guidance of her Feng Shui books, she had worked on the areas of Money, Fame and Relationship, but nothing seemed to change, she was not finding the happiness that she had hoped for.

That is when I entered her scene, she asked me to take a look at her home. I knew what the Calling was, and I knew the best places for her to work in the house, I had done my readings. So we went into the area of LAKE in her house, and I asked her questions about childhood and her creativity. She said, "*There was little space to be a child, I carried a great deal of responsibility, I was groomed to be the big girl, I took the role of being grown up, responsible and useful. I even felt responsible for the well-being of my parents and my big sister. My mother used to put my hair up in tight buns and curls, so this is the image I carried, and I felt so restricted in it.*"

She carried this image of herself into adulthood, her self-esteem relied upon it, only now is she beginning to drop it. She knows she has carried too much, she was the youngest daughter, so it was not even her place to take such responsibility.

'Being an anchor in a community' was her role in the family and also the vocation she chose. So many people rely upon her now; she is a good mother, a good teacher and a good healer, always the source of good advice.

In the reading it says: *"Each person as a link is critical to all the others, but your anchor is the one that holds them together. You will best serve the people around you by cultivating your own character. Although they must rely on you, your position is equal to theirs – in them you will find the complement of your own nature, so your personal development is linked with those who are drawn to this union, and each one holds a key to the development of the others. Allow others to be who they are, so they may find their own way."*

Tracking back across the plan, we went to look at THUNDER. Influences are strong between the opposites and the diagonals of the plan. Thunder is where we pick up the script and become the author of our own life stories, we take in the experiences, we accept the conditions, and we grow up. The influences in our lives go back a long way, way back to our ancestors. It is in THUNDER that we are gifted to become our own authority, and it is in THUNDER that we are given heavy loads to bear. So this is the area of the plan that relates to Diana's grooming and conditioning, her taking the role of being so responsible, especially in relation to the well being of her older sister, a role that was out of place with her age and position in the family.

We sat and talked in her THUNDER area. She told me that she felt an ancestral connection; she felt that there were things buried in her family's past that she was carrying. It was cold in Diana's house, so she warmed herself in front of the open fire. Looking at the fire we were drawn into conversation about its qualities, and I told her of an area in the plan that holds these fire qualities. It was the area she called 'Fame'. It is to do with recognition, but more than this it holds the qualities of clarity, truth, and love. I walked her through the area of FIRE, and illustrated how the Fire energy in her house was not contained, it did not really have a place. In her house FIRE was a small area that joined the kitchen with the hallway and the sitting room, a place one passes through on the way to somewhere else. Curiously also, she did not have any proper heating in the house, when it got really cold they wrapped blankets around themselves, and in the evenings they huddled around the open fire. Not because she could not afford heating, but because she had chosen to spend money on other things, such as laminate flooring in the bedrooms, which would now have to be taken up if central heating was to be installed. So Fire in the home was an issue for her.

Recognition was an issue for her, and so was clarity, but the biggest issue was Love. She looked very sad, and told me of a relationship she had lost, it had all become a bit entangled, they both had issues that got in the way. From what I had said about family and ancestral influences in THUNDER, she thought this was the root of their relationship problems. As she said this she remembered an old armchair catching fire in the THUNDER area of her house.

This was an aha! Moment. I knew it was relevant, and so I wanted to see where it would take us, I said: *"An armchair is a place where you are with yourself, quite unlike a sofa which you share with others – It is your place."* Diana also felt sure there was something significant about the burning of the old chair. She said: *"My son woke up in the middle of the night, he was having a bad dream, and that is how we discovered the burning smell. The chair was black and smouldering so I picked up the cushions and threw them outside, and then put the chair frame on top. Within an hour there was a sudden flash, which we saw from the bedroom window. The chair had gone up in flames, and in the morning there was nothing left, just a small pile of black soot. I thought at the time that something ancestral had cleared - we had a really lucky escape."*

So we returned to the THUNDER area to look at the armchair she was now using. It was an old wooden chair that she had restored, it was painted bright orange, and she really liked it. It seemed to me that the best place for this chair would be in MOUNTAIN, only a move of a few feet, but a significant placement in the story of her life.

MOUNTAIN is the place where we are at peace with ourselves,

happy and well grounded in our own company. When we are not in touch with MOUNTAIN, we are easily moved by the influence of others.

She said of the MOUNTAIN area, *"It has always been very busy and full up. Now it has the dining table, and before that it had the big sofa, and I have no time or space to do creative and playful things for myself."*

With this statement she had made the link between MOUNTAIN and LAKE – always being so useful to other people, she filled her life up in this way, and this took energy away from her creativity. What she missed in childhood she was still missing in adulthood. So knocking through the wall in LAKE and placing her orange armchair in MOUNTAIN were both very good ideas, but LAKE had to be worked on before MOUNTAIN. She had to get the right piece of the jigsaw puzzle in place before the other pieces would fit.

The idea to move her armchair just a few feet would effect every other area, and all the changes she wanted to make would now fall into place. The dining table would go into the HEAVEN area, making this the family room, so the garage would become the treatment room, and FIRE would become the study.

To allow all of this to happen, the masonry wall in LAKE would have to be knocked down. Diana now talks of knocking down the wall as her 'breakthrough'.. She says, *"In bashing through LAKE I was saying I am taking some space for myself."* When the time came to demolish the wall, she approached the builders and asked them if she could do it herself. So they gave her the sledgehammer and stood back to watch. She was so embarrassed, striking the wall as hard as she could was not making any impact, and the builders were watching in amusement. Then in a good-hearted way they gave her a lesson on how to do it. When the job was complete so many areas of her home benefited, and she began to establish better boundaries in her personal life.

HEAVEN and EARTH now felt more connected, and the new study area in FIRE became a hub for all the family. Diana said: *"Before it was a walkway, very insignificant, now it has become a hub for all the family. I have photos of all the people I love in there, it is now an area we all use a lot, FIRE in the house is in a good space because it feels more held. I have still not got around to putting a door on it, I am a bit unsure about a door, perhaps I don't want to contain the FIRE too much, that might make it stagnant."*

Working on FIRE, decorating it and sorting it out, she got more clarity about her life. Her son decided to go away to boarding school, she found more time and space for herself, and a new man entered her love life. But not for long – between her son in boarding school, her lover in another part of the country, and other commitments at home and work, she was driving all over the place. Then one morning when pulling out of her driveway, she was hit by another car. Whiplash from the accident forced her to take time out, she could not do anything else, no driving, no working, and no taking care of other people. She spent lots of time just lying down, alone in her own space, and felt that this was what she really needed, through keeping still she was becoming more centred.

In this condition she found some inner peace and inner space, and this she connected with the UNITY area of her house, so she wanted the partitions to be taken down in this area. These partitions formed a cupboard under the stair, and even though removing them would expose an uneven floor and make the coats and shoes more visible, the thought of this made her happier. So when her son came home from boarding school she got him to do this for her. In this year when she had to give up working and doing so much, Diana made progress along the line of THUNDER/UNITY/LAKE. Having cleared so much she entered into a new relationship with herself, which took her back to MOUNTAIN, to the place where 'relationship with oneself' is the key issue.

In the consultation, I did not talk about all the areas of her house in detail, we basically followed one story line that led us from LAKE into THUNDER, then into FIRE, and back to THUNDER, which led to MOUNTAIN. At the end of the consultation I told Diana some things to look out for in the future.

In the area of WIND there was a picture of two cherubs on the wall, the smaller cherub had its arm around the bigger cherub as if taking care of her. Beneath the picture was an old cabinet, and so I enquired about its contents. Diana said it was filled with wedding presents from her marriage, they were not things that she wanted any more, but they were hard to give away. She looked at the cherub picture and said she had a mug with exactly the same image on it. She realized: "*It represents me looking after my sister.*" Clearly it did. Eleven months after the consultation Diana made her breakthrough in LAKE, and behind the scenes this stirred things up and she had a big conflict with her sister. She took the cherub picture off the wall and tore it in half, and in her anger she smashed the cherub mug. She had the door blocked up that went through WIND to FIRE, where the cherub picture used to be, and she gave the cabinet and all the wedding presents away to people she thought would appreciate them. She felt that all those things held her in the past, in out of date dysfunctional ways of relating.

When Diana sorted out the FIRE area she cleared up a lot of things, but it took her two more years to get around to sorting out the central heating. Two years later, just at the time when the plumbers began the central heating work, her sister was at a very low place in her life, so Diana invited her to move in for a short time until she could get back on her feet. So Diana moved her armchair out of MOUNTAIN and replaced it with a sofa big enough for them all to sit on. Then her son quit school and moved back home, so many more people began to call.

Realizing what she had done, Diana moved the big sofa back to where it was before and returned her own bright orange armchair back to the MOUNTAIN place, and with this gesture she created more space and stillness in her life once more.

Diana said: "*My sister came to live with me when I was finally sorting out the FIRE energy in the house. I gave her a room but she never occupied it, she was unable to take her place and floated from room to room. For ten weeks it was very challenging for me, but when she left she had really found her feet, and this gave me a great feeling of joy and relaxation to see her moving on in a new and empowered direction. Now I am going to get a really comfy chair for my Mountain, I want to chill out there, and I want to put a really long sofa in Wind and Thunder as a space for everyone to be comfortable. Now I feel settled in relationships in a way that I have never felt before. If you were to say to me what is your big issue now? I haven't really got one. I have had a big expansion in consciousness around relationships and money. I had to get off the hamster wheel to find this space, so now I have extended the mortgage and I am looking at ways of investing in myself, and making my investments work. I feel that my whole programming with money is completely changing around this time. The homesouls readings have given me tremendous courage to do what I want, they seem to come from somewhere special."*

Diana's house is now warm and feels really settled. She is about to replace the open fire with a new wood burning stove, and this coincides with her decision to invest in herself and to become a family therapist, using creative expression as the vehicle to turn relationships around, what was once her problem, has become her wonderful opportunity.

Some points I would like to highlight about Diana's consultation:

Knowing where to look

Diana's story shows that issues are not in one place. Issues are connected like a web across the plan, and when you work in one area of the plan, you pull the strings in another. However, I always recommend not spreading oneself too far afield. To work in one place at a time is usually enough; sometimes it may be necessary to work in two, but hardly ever should we take on more than this. I don't mean that complete house renovations are never called for, what I mean to say is do not give your energy to issues in more than one or two places at a time.

Choosing where to start

Sometimes the area that needs your attention is obvious, perhaps there are leaking pipes, or it is an area of your house that you dislike, or something really bothers you about it.

Diana knew intuitively that the area she needed to work on was LAKE, and she knew she had to take the wall down. What she did not know was why, and that is where the readings in this book helped her. I asked the Oracle which area Diana should work on first, and I picked the Turquoise Rune, which is LAKE. So if you do not know which area in your house to work on, you can do the same – just pick a Glass Rune.

Looking for the clue

Now you know where to look, you may be wondering what to look for. Something about the place is calling for your attention; something reflects an image of an issue you need to work on. In Diana's case there was the separating wall in LAKE, the cherub picture in WIND, the armchair in MOUNTAIN, and the lack of heating was reflective of issues in FIRE. If you need some help to focus, you could do a reading from chapter 4, asking: *'What is the main issue in this area of my home?'*

To read your space you will have to use your imagination, for help with this refer to Chapter 3: *The Ambience – How the space feels, The Story – What the space says, The ingredients – What the space needs.*

When you find the clue, what do you do?

I cannot tell you what to do when I do not know what it is you will find. This is not like Feng Shui, where there are standard remedies or cures.

The breakthrough for Diana in LAKE was knocking the wall down. In WIND it was blocking up the door, and removing the cherub picture. In MOUNTAIN it was making this a quiet place with a nice armchair instead of the dining table.

Each action was dictated by the image of the problem. Something will be Calling you, but sometimes you will not be able to see it. If this is the case then simply transform something about the space to make it feel and look much better, perhaps tidy it up, or make it smell nice, deal with a job that you have been putting off for some time, or put some flowers in the area. You must decide what seems most appropriate. Finding the right place, working with the right image, and doing something positive are all-important, but most of all it is your Intention that makes the biggest difference.

How do you interpret what something means?
There is no standard way. The question is, what does the image mean to you? Trust your imagination to take you somewhere, follow your nose, and like a treasure hunt one clue will lead to another.

Not all images need to be explored
There were lots of things in Diana's house, but we did not consider them all. Only certain things captured our attention and some things we found did not need to be dealt with right away. The cherub picture and mug for instance did not come into focus until twelve months after the consultation, when Diana knocked the wall down.

The process of deconstruction is not so much analysis, for if we dissect, take apart, we remain on the outside looking in, we do not then enter the image. We enter the image as if we are entering the theatre, to see where its story takes us, to follow wherever it leads.

We are surrounded by images all of the time. Most of the time we should let them be, it would not do to trouble ourselves with the meaning of so many things, but sometimes circumstances in our lives call for more attention, if not for action then at least for contemplation.

Remember that interpretations are always fantasies, no matter what you believe, life is always built on fantasy. Each of us has a unique life story that makes us who we are. Behind the scenes in the magic of the imagination, your images work with you, so find the image that needs attention – that fits your story at this moment in time, and journey with the image in your own way.

Sometimes it won't be easy, time and again something will catch your eye and you will know there is a message in it for you, but you won't be able to pin it down. This part of the journey calls for some soul searching and keeps you awake to the mystery of life.

The journey back to the center may take a whole lifetime, and when we get there we may hope to reflect upon a life well lived. So many people measure a successful life by what has been achieved in the world of appearances, but surely the real measure of a good life is how well it has been received and shared as a gift for all to benefit from. The landscape is infinite and eternal, but the journey may not take you further than your home. Everything you need comes to you on this journey when you are open and receptive. The wisdom that exists beyond the veil will push lessons your way and it will pull you towards them. The purpose of this Oracle is not to teach but to guide. It will help you to find your own treasures hidden in the details of your home. We are all explorers.

In the words of TS Eliot:

> *"We shall not cease from exploration*
> *And the end of all our exploring*
> *Will be to arrive where we started from*
> *And know the place for the first time."*

The Calling – Following your story line

Our lives are intimately linked with the lives of others, even with people and places we have not yet met or discovered. It is as if some sort of light works outside our chronological time, paving the way and clearing the space so we may enter. Along the storyline the scene is set ahead of time, and you are somewhere along the line right now.

Your story precedes you, intimately linked with other people's lives and other people's places, and in time you will inherit what they need to pass on. When you move into a new place, look into the details of the place, for you will find that some of your issues are already there. When the time comes to move, you feel it, you no longer fit the circumstances you live in, and you feel that somewhere else is calling you. We know our place when we find it, somehow we manage to navigate there and intuitively the place feels just right.

Some people move house prematurely, thinking they can sweep their issues under the carpet, moving to escape the things that are going wrong. I have seen this often, and I know that issues not resolved in one place will often follow people around from one house to the next.

Like a chap I met a few years ago; he had taken advice from a renowned Feng Shui Master, who told him to move house because the EARTH area was missing and this was responsible for his failing relationships. So he moved, and in his next house his relationships failed again, so he moved again. Clearly the EARTH issues were following him around. Failed relationships were part of his story, and until he stayed put to face up to what his home was showing him, the issues would continue to follow him around.

The main issues in our lives will always call for attention, they cannot be hidden or brushed away, they linger in the details; in the blocked drains and the leaking taps, in the unfinished jobs and items that need repair, in the attics, basements, cupboards and under the stairs. We may ask ourselves: 'What is in the picture on the wall and the ornament on the window? What secret does it hold? What story can it tell?' And 'What if I was to alter my home: to repaint it or to extend some part of it, or pull a bit down; what would this say about my life? Is this what is called for?'

We may dialogue with the details of our homes, for there is therapeutic value in seeing the home as a mirror of self. As we become conscious of the way the home reflects our sub-conscious issues, we act as physicians, working homoeopathically; for everything in the home holds a memory and carries a message: every object, action, and thought can be healing.

Life Themes

Know it or not, like it or not, there are themes that run through your life. There are themes that have run from the beginning of time right through to you in this moment: family themes, cultural themes and personal themes, story lines that link you to the conditions of the past and influence you in the present. These themes run right through our lives, we can trace their story in the body and the home, they play away in the background pulling our strings, animating our actions and influencing the course that life will take. We are all puppets, until we realise that we can pull the strings ourselves. We can follow them back to their source; we can bless them, cut them, and let them go. We can grasp them, pull them and let them flow, or accept them and let them be. We travel along these story lines, knowingly or not, playing along with them, these conditional threads that influence the way we think and act, that tie us to our family, culture and tribe.

You can pick up the trail in your home, for every place and every thing in that place is a clue leading you to the source that pulls your strings. The journey is a treasure hunt to find what is affecting the story of your life and to gain some insight into how this may be changed.

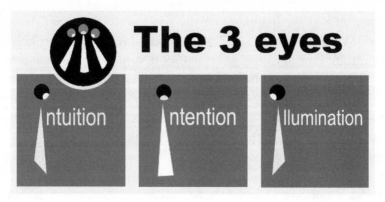

The way you see the world is the way it is.
Change your view, then your experience will change too.

The essence of life flows like sap from the Source through the root and into the passing stream of image and experience.

We channel it and the invisible becomes manifest in the world. Moved and stirred by the strength of the flow, we shape our vision and set the course for our experience.

We gather what comes from our depths and we pass it on, putting it out there, illuminating our experience for beauty to shine in the form of what we create.

We live through the act of creation.

Homesouls in a designer's eye is engaged with a process of building for Soul. To do this we have to become more creative with perception and more open to inspiration. I have named the process the three eyes. **Intuition** is the survey, **Intention** is the brief, **Illumination** is the building process.

Intuition takes us to the source, through the roots of our experience, opening the way for inspiration and ideas to flow. The space we move in holds all we need to know. We need only pay attention to what is with us at each moment, for the answers to our questions are always close by, hidden in the details of our stories and our homes.

Nourish the root to enjoy the fruit: **Tune in, Contemplate, Meditate, Dream and Imagine.**

Intention gives things a place in the world, and consolidates our stories. Thoughts that are motivated with intent gather form to take shape in this world.

When a thought comes, you have a choice; you can let it go and it will recede, or you can do something with it – you can ground it and help it to grow. As soon as you affirm an intention, you empower a thought and motivate your energy to follow it.

It helps to write your intention down, to give it presence in your physical world. Sometimes a good intention is all you need to manifest changes in your life:

Consider, consolidate, and compose.

Illumination. Sometimes a good intention is not sufficient to bring about change; more dedication is needed, there is work to be done. Illuminate your experience so that meaning shines through in the form of what you do. Whatever you do – make it glorious, for your acts of creation are everyday prayers. Once you put your heart into something, providence moves with you. You may light a candle, put up a picture or clean out a corner; this is your **Invocation**, your **Dedication** and your **Call for Change**.

Intuition

The Survey - Contemplate, Meditate, Dream and Imagine.
When I say Intuition, I mean 'to survey', to look and to listen, to tune into what is there. Intuition to me means to be in-tuition, but the education is very deep, there are often no visible teachers, the classroom tends to be wherever we happen to be, and the instruction comes from whatever is there.

When instinctively you know where in your home to look, or what to deal with, you are In-tuition, being guided.

When you choose Glass Runes to give you a reading or to direct you where to look this is In-tuition too. But who or what is guiding? I sense a presence and I name it Soul.

To be creative is a Calling, a heartfelt Calling of the Soul to put us in touch with all creation.

In the home we are in-tuition, we are novices in a theatre of Soul. We need to practice, to do the homework, to be awake to what is happening in our lives, to look and listen, to be open for the clues, and to follow our clues as a journey that will lead us where we need to go. Sometimes the clue is obvious, but its meaning might not be so visible, so we have to journey deeper.

As I write this, I have a WATER issue; that this is the problem is obvious. Our water pipe to the fields is leaking, so we have to carry buckets over to the animals, and the oil supply to our boiler is leaking in the ground outside the house, so the smell of oil is contaminating the taste of our water. Our water is a metered supply, we pay for every drop, and oil is very expensive, so we are literally wasting money with every drip. We have three showers, and for various reasons, none of them are working properly and the waste pipes to our wash basins and sinks all need clearing.

Now I can deal with all of these practical problems, and the nature of the problem is obviously WATER, so I need a plumber. But clearly there is something else going on in my life right now and a plumber will not sort this out for me. The issues that concern me most at the moment are to do with 'Financial Investment' and 'Time'. Just how much time do I have to expand my homesouls work, and how much money do I need to raise to build the new homesouls office and teaching space and to set up the new website and office facility? If you turn to the keywords for WATER, in Scene 1 of Chapter 2, you will see that 'Investment' and 'Time' are WATER issues. So intuitively I know that my practical water problems are a reflection of my Time/Investment issues. I am In-tuition about these issues, knowing that there is something to be learned about this situation.

In Chapter 1, I talked about going into the problem through its image, or symptom. The images for me now are leaking and blocked pipes. I can fix these, but whilst the Investment/Time issue is still current, WATER problems will continue to surface.

In seeing the connection, I am already entering the looking glass – looking behind the scenes, and through this recognition, the wheels of change are set in motion. But I have to do more than just look. I know I have to get to the bottom of this. Whilst fixing the pipes, I am aware of the bigger picture. And by working on the problem, I know that behind the scenes the bigger picture will also change, and I have to change with it.

So what do I need to know here? I ask the homesouls Oracle, and this is what its says:

HEAVEN/EARTH   (White/Yellow) "Attunement and Co-ordination"

Heaven and Earth are out of communion

These runes call you at a time when certain parts of your life are breaking apart or breaking down, and you feel torn. There is no quick fix and nothing to be gained by continuing this way or by maintaining this status quo. Action is called for, but first you must bide your time to establish inner calm. Fate will show the way. Just be open, patient and persevering, then co-ordinate your whole being to work in harmony with the time, to do what must be done.

Inner and outer voices influence your life, pulling you this way and that, rocking your boat until you do not know the way to go. Soul calls to you to follow your true path. Your ego and some of the people in your life ask you to make some bad decisions and you are torn between your affections, your duties and associations. Your sacred calling is personal to you, it does not call you to please the others or follow their path; it calls for you to go your own way and to be your own life coach. Soul knows the people and the places where you belong, and will guide you to the company of good companions and good advice. You may suffer loss along the way, so be it! Stand your ground – be brave – stand up for what you believe in and withdraw from what is wrong. Expect to encounter internal and external conflict by going this way, for you rock the status quo in the circle of family, friends and acquaintances.

This reading takes me closer, before the reading there was so much possibility. The Glass Runes are like glass doors, and each reading is like a room, once you are in there, you are much closer to the issue in your life, you have entered the looking glass. The reading does not give me a specific answer; it focuses my attention on certain aspects of my issue that I need to make some choices about.

I can see one very clear reflection of *Heaven and Earth being out of communion.* For two months now my head has been in the writing of this book. Focussed on the script, sifting back through old consultations and nit picking through the details, I have not taken much exercise over the past two months, I have neglected the outside work, my office is a mess, and without much help from me, Jackie has not been able to keep on top of our domestic situation.

This is not the way I intend to carry on, so we are going to have to make some good choices, so that Heaven and Earth can be in communion in our lives, and the Journey of our lives can continue to flow with ease. So as from tomorrow I will start to fix the Water problems, and whilst I am doing this I will think about the bigger issues in hand.

More often, an issue or a problem is not so immediately apparent, or not so much in need of immediate attention. Things come up, come into our awareness, they catch our attention, and are with us for a while, they enter the imagination and we journey with them into further understanding. In this respect there is a big difference between homesouls and Feng Shui.

Feng Shui jumps into action too soon, without enough reflection. It is through reflection that we enter the looking glass. Intuition takes us into the reflection, we enter the image, and we journey through the window into Soul.

Currently I am involved with a group of friends on a journey around the wheel of changes, taking a look at each element in turn. Last night we met to discuss what is going on for us in this element of WATER. I told them my story about the water pipes and the oil, and one friend told us what is going on for him. He told us about an aspect of himself, that he has difficulty accepting. He has visualised this part of himself: it has a face, it is a child, and he finds its image disturbing (for now I will call this an 'inner child'). Occasionally something will happen in my friend's life that prompts him to recall this image. Until recently his response has been to cast the image aside, to disown it, a few nights ago, however, he pictured this inner child in his home, he imagined caring for it, placing it in the bath and washing it. He asked me if this seems like a WATER issue. He happened to be sitting in the WATER area of his home whilst telling us his story, and we were all

facing him. A picture on the wall behind him caught my eye, and I asked him to take it down, so that we could all look at it.

The painting is called *"Melencolia"*, painted by Albrecht Durer. We were all struck by the imagery and how well it fitted the story he had been telling us, but he looked at the painting and said that it did not strike a chord in him, that he had never given this painting much thought. So I asked him: What can you see in it now? He studied the painting for a moment, then talked about what he could see. His eyes surveyed all around the painting, describing the objects at the edges and the angel to the right of centre. Ten minutes passed and not once did he mention the small child right in the middle of the painting. The small child was the first thing the rest of us noticed, but he was not going to see it. In fact, he said, "I just did not see it".

Often what we need to know is right there, staring us right in the face, but we do not see it, our perception is blinkered. Perhaps it has to be this way, when something deep within the story needs to be stirred we need an epiphany, a revelation, something that makes the eyes light up as we exclaim aha! A defining point in time, that we will not forget. As if once blinded, now we see. This is how it was for my friend when we pointed to the child in the middle of the painting. He can now see his own reflection in this painting, an aspect of himself that he wants to look at. The painting is now a window through which he can enter the scene into which this disowned aspect of himself is cast.

I have given you plenty of examples of images that hold the story of an issue that's calling for attention. In Esther's home there was the painting of Hylas and the Nymphs, and the missing area of Heaven. In Diana's home there was the wall she wanted to demolish and the burning armchair. And you will come to Anne's story soon. In Anne's home there is her grandfather's cabinet, and her lovers *Lovespoon* next to the mother and baby giraffe on the mantle above the fireplace. Each client and friend I have mentioned, used their imagination to enter the story, to begin a journey into the image, seeing through the looking glass.

What area will you look at now? If you have not already done so, then choose one area of your home. You might have practical reasons for wanting to look at a particular area; you may already know which area is calling for your attention. Your intuition may be guiding you there, or you could choose your area by taking one Glass Rune from the Bag.

ORANGE WIND	RED FIRE	YELLOW EARTH
GREEN THUNDER	CLEAR UNITY	TURQUOISE LAKE
PURPLE MOUNTAIN	BLUE WATER	WHITE HEAVEN

Take a close look at your chosen area, ask yourself questions. It is best to write your answers in your home journal, as a permanent record that you might want to refer to in the future.

- What is the first thing that comes to mind about this area?
- Write down all the other things that come to mind.
- How does it make you feel?
- What needs doing here?
- What things aren't you happy with?

- What do you love about this place?
- Do you know any stories about this area?
- What is the story behind each of the things in this area?
- If this area could speak what would it say?
- And what would you say to it?

"What issue should I work on in this area of my home?"

Now you have looked closely, the issue may be clear to you. If it is not clear then ask the homesouls Oracle. Think of the above question and choose Glass Runes for the reading:

With your eyes closed take one Glass Rune from the bag (remember the colour), put it back, shake the bag then take another.

These two Runes in the order you chose them will give you a reading. Refer to the Readings Index in Chapter 4 then turn to your reading for guidance on the meaning of these two runes.

You may be content to work on the bigger picture, simply nourishing this space as if you were nourishing this issue in your life, that is often all you need to do. Some people will want to look more deeply, to find the reflection of their issue in their space. Can you find it there? Is it reflected in the way the space feels, or the jobs that need doing, in the pictures on the wall or the mess that needs clearing up? Is it reflected in the way that people use this space or the way that it is neglected? Is it in the view out of the window or in the furniture and things that are stored here? Where is it? Sometimes the story is obvious, sometimes it is staring you right in the face, but you cannot see it; and sometimes you will have to use a bit more imagination.

Intention

The Brief - Consider, Consolidate, Compose.

So we enter our story through Intuition, to Journey behind the scene, following a clue along a storyline that leads to an insight or a new perception. Sometimes realisation and perception are enough to spark a change in one's life, realising something we have not seen before or seeing something in a new way changes something within the scene, and life is different than before. Often, more work is needed; we might perceive what we want but a call for change needs more grounding. Inspirations, insights and realisations are light and airy, they have no gravity, they are not really here, we need to give them weight to make them work.

To form an Intention is to be clear about what you are Calling for. It helps to write something down, and to make it concise. If you have started a home journal, as I suggested in Chapter 1, you should by now be finding it very useful. It helps you to consolidate your thoughts and ground your intuitions; it helps you to see the patterns in the web, and to be able to look back over the clues that you have found and the links that you have made. By writing an idea down, it becomes present in the world, it is no longer floating about in space; you give it a place, bringing it closer to you.

So if you are Calling for something, make your Intention an affirmation of what you really want, but be careful what you ask for – remember Esther's story, when she asked for "a good Christian", she got a good man called 'Christian', and he was not available for her. Perhaps she was too specific, not leaving the door open enough for destiny and fate to work together on her issue. Try not to turn Intentions into a shopping list, as you will probably get what you ask for, but it might not be what you really want.

Often we do not know what we really want; we just want help and guidance to find our way through an issue. Jackie's story at the end of this chapter is an example of this. She knew what she did not want, and in looking for her own 'North Star', her intent was to be wakeful and watchful to the scene unfolding, so she did some readings to bring more clarity and focus to her point of view. Sometimes we need to go more with the flow, as Jackie did in her story, and sometimes we need to take the driving seat, as Diana did when she made her breakthrough by knocking down the wall.

Intention is a powerful thing; sometimes it is all we need to resolve a problematic issue. Clients often say that when they phoned to make an appointment with me, immediately after the phone call they felt something shift in their lives. Some have stories of the unusual events that unfolded, and some say that by the time of my arrival the weight they were carrying had lifted.

When considering your Intention, choose your words carefully, there is magic in this process and it is wise to take care in what you ask for. Are you asking for what you really want? Are your Intentions honorable?

One of the most powerful men in Welsh mythology was a poet called 'Taliesen'. He was employed by the Kings of old to speak the words that would bring power to their leadership, and through his words enemies would fall. This might be a bit far-fetched for the modern mind, but central to this story is the power of the word.

In our acts of creation first there is Intuition and then Intention. In the beginning was the word, or so it is said in Genesis: "*And the spirit of God moved upon the face of the waters. And God said, Let there be light: and there was light.*"

Something Divine moves within our lives. We call and the Divine answers our call. Good Intentions are heard, but actions demonstrate more commitment, and with commitment, providence moves too. In the home our actions speak louder than words, so use your imagination for design to make your life an everyday prayer.

Illumination

The Building Process – Invocation, Dedication, Call for Change

> *What you see around you is a reflection of who you are.*
> *So create the change you want to see in the world.*
> *Paint your picture – your home is your canvas.*
> *Walk your talk – your life is your journey home.*

You are not alone in this endeavour, all our roads lead to the same space, all our minds inhabit the same space, and we all share the same font of healing, memory and imagination from which inspiration springs. Its source is the home of Soul where all are connected, each one part of a greater whole. With each move, each act and each thought, Soul's space is stirred and something shifts for everyone.

We each have a unique way of placing ourselves in the world, of setting the scene to serve our lives. There are many ways of seeing and many things to believe in, so we choose to filter before we accept, to let the mind open to thoughts and beliefs that fit the concepts we construct for our lives. We shut out and cast off the things that do not fit. We colour our lives in different ways – through different coloured lenses we perceive the world. Some may see through rose-coloured glass, taking an optimistic view, seeing the happy side of life, or seeing things the way they want them to be. Some colour it green with envy, blue with melancholy, pristine white and holier-than-thou, or black with sombre mood. There are so many moods through which we can filter our experience and so many colours with which one could choose to paint the scene. The way you see and how you filter is entirely up to you. Colour your world the way you want it to be. Through the space beyond your place, Soul comes knocking at your door, so open the channel. Let every aspect of interior design become a statement of intent and a request for something special in your life.

The homesouls journey begins at home with who you are and how you place yourself amongst your things. All around you life is colored in a beautiful way. You may not see it, it may not appear that way from your point of view. Looks can be deceptive, for beauty touches the heart – it needn't be appealing to the eye. Our homes need not be pictorially beautiful, aesthetically pleasing and squeaky clean. Our homes are mirrors of ourselves.

On this homesouls journey you have already asked yourself: Who am I? What ails me? And how do I want things to be? You have entered the scene and entered the Wound. You have begun the work of de-construction.

Now it is time to create the change you want to see in your life, building the home of Soul, shaping your world through your true image, doing the work to bring new thoughts down to earth and to ground them in the way things are.

Put your heart into this work, for whatever you put into it will motivate the outcome. **Intuition** is the survey, **Intention** is the brief, **Illumination** is the building process.

To reconstruct symbolically a part of your life that needs rebuilding, maintenance or repair, first you need to prepare your space: Clear the site, get rid of the clutter and clean it. You have to make some room for something new to enter. Your preparations welcome the new.

Several years ago Jackie and I decided to have a good clear-out. We filled a few big bags with things that no longer seemed to fit our lives: clothes that didn't fit, toys the kids had grown out of, books we had read, ornaments and pictures that no longer inspired us. I took them to the goodwill shop and said to Jackie: "Now we have created a vacuum, I wonder what new stuff will try to rush in!"

Jackie went out for the day and returned home with a friend, carrying two big bags. I had to laugh, and not very tactfully added: "I wondered where all the stuff would come from." This stuff was what our friends were getting rid of. Some of it they thought might be suitable for us.

Nature will fill an empty space – it doesn't like a vacuum. I know this from working on my land. I know that if I do not pull up the brambles and get the sheep in to graze, the place will become overgrown.

It's the same in the house, things accumulate like weeds and our lives become tangled and overgrown. In the home as in the garden, if we don't keep the place clear of weeds, the things we want to grow will suffer. We have to make choices about what we want to fill our space with. Our friends were being kind, but this was not the stuff we had cleared our space for. We were not looking for more material things; we were longing for something else. We didn't know what, but we were content to have a clear space and wait with an open mind and an open heart.

We are all attached to everything we own: every piece of paper, every book and every object, all the things we have stored up in the attic or in the garage and the spare room, and all the presents we feel obliged to keep. Our attachments are like threads connecting us to the people, places and things that form the context of our lives. Too many attachments are like overgrown brambles sucking nourishment from fertile ground. Freed from these attachments we feel a sense of release, a feeling of lightness accompanies the clearing process.

We have been rebuilding our home and our farm for twelve years now; one small job every year at first, and then a major rebuild and extension. We have made places we love to be in, and in each room everything has a place. We surround ourselves with the things we love and make a place for the really useful things as well. Some of our things are not beautiful or useful, but they are meaningful and that is why they are there. The really useful things need a suitable place so practical storage and organization is an important part of my design.

As I come to the end of this book I am drawing close to completing my home. We are now working on the FIRE area. It holds issues of completion, recognition, beauty, love, passion, fun and truth. Writing this book and the rebuilding of my home have been intimately connected. They were both started around the same time. The journey has been turbulent and we have worked through a mess for some of the time, but that's okay, our house is not a machine for living in but the vessel we journey through life in.

Now there is much more order, we feel more settled and content, but we look back with romantic eyes to the time when the children were growing in a small house overfilled with things. Now we can see the beauty that was growing in our chaos and how we prospered our nature and tended the garden of the Soul in the place we call our home.

This is not the way it needs to be for everyone, it is just the route our path took. We took the high road and climbed a mountain and we did it by ourselves. I would not recommend this to anyone else, unless they feel compelled to go this way. We must all journey at our own pace, and I recommend working with one place and one issue, one step at time. My home needed some demolition and rebuilding, and this creative, constructive process helped consolidate this book. Most homes just need some maintenance and care.

Too much order can undermine creativity, becoming obsessive and blocking the flow that leads to flowering. Beauty, it seems, will flower in chaos, but there is a time for flowering and a time for clearing away, as nature shows us in the summer and the fall.

I don't pay much attention to the fashion police, or the beautiful body and beautiful home magazines. The gloss is pulled over the designer's eye, this veil of illusion makes them blind, and the blind lead the blind in this designer-land of little substance.

I look beyond the surface in search of beauty and poetry. The Welsh poet Dylan Thomas knew this well, throughout his life he drew inspiration from his hometown Swansea, the place he called his "ugly lovely town".

In its ugliness and its loveliness your home can nourish your life. The healing process is the same as the creative process. Engaged in the act of creation we seem at first to make a mess, and when the body is healing the symptoms often get worse before the condition gets better. A similar thing happens at home when we clear our space.

I sometimes think of the home like a cauldron in which we mix the ingredients that nourish and shape our lives. All the ingredients of life's story are in this vessel and when we stir things up what we need rises to the surface. If there are blocks and bars to movement, the stirring will bring up the key. Sometimes doors will open to the strangest places, old wounds may open and old issues resurface, needing healing and clearing in your own way.

Before we build, we deconstruct, dismantle, sift through and clear. Once you have cleared your space then it is time to make your design a glorious statement of who you are, what you feel and what you want in life. The clearing I have been talking about is very practical. It involves going through your things and dealing with them in a way that seems fitting. The way you deal with your things is part of the transformation process. Recycle things if you can. Burn or bin the rubbish, but anything that sparks a recollection or fires your imagination calls for a moment of contemplation – what does this thing mean in your life and what is the best way for you to deal with it?

In 1996 I decided to give up my practice as an architect, and instead to focus fulltime on my homesouls work, which in those days I called *Hiraeth*. It required faith and commitment not only to give up a lucrative vocation, but also to let go of the image of architect, a part of my identity that no longer needed to play the leading role. I piled up the trappings of my profession and paused for a moment in front of the pyre, contemplating the most appropriate words and ceremony, but all I did was strike a match and turn my back on the burning. I walked away and this seemed appropriate.

The fire burned for three days, and out of the blue a phone call came from the RIBA (Royal Institute of British Architects), asking me to give a talk on Feng Shui to inform the profession. I sent them a draft but they clearly didn't like what I had to say. That was the first and the last time I heard from the RIBA. The contact was poetic and just, and I was happy with the burning and with the phoenix that rose from the fire.

Sometimes it is not enough to have a ceremonial fire, it is necessary to deal with the issue before you can let it go: someone may need to be contacted, someone may need forgiveness and goodwill. Some things you have forgotten may need resurrecting.

I find it best to act like THUNDER in my clearing: clean-sweeping an area, getting rid of the bulk quickly with energy and enthusiasm.

When THUNDER approaches we feel it in the air, we feel the pressure building and then the clap bursts with sudden shock and sweeps across the land. After the passing the air feels lighter, and this is how I feel after the initial surge of clearing away. With this surge of energy I can move on to tackle the more difficult matters.

Practical clearing is fundamental, but some may feel it is not enough. There are many ways to clear a space: clapping, drumming, ringing bells and chanting are just a few. Karen Kingston has covered these in her book: *Creating Sacred Space with*

Feng Shui.

To clear the energy in my house before redecorating, we paint a symbol on the walls, and in the paint we mix a '*Tachyon*' powder called 'stardust'. I cannot say conclusively how this works, but I can really feel the difference it makes, giving each room a sense of lightness and clarity. For more about 'stardust', visit the website www.homesouls.com

So now you have been creative in your clearing, it is time to get busy with construction, decoration and placement.

This is not a book about design, it is a book about entering your story, reading your home, and creating the changes that you want in your life. Inevitably design issues will come up, and many of my clients have relied upon my experience as

This symbol came to Jackie several years ago. She took it to mean as in Heaven so on Earth

an architect to help them find good design solutions. But the danger in giving design ideas here, is that they might be taken as prescriptions. In this book, I am not telling you what you need to do. I am not giving you prescriptions. I want you to engage your own imagination. In this homesouls work there are no formulas or prescriptions, we are all uniquely different, and with a little help and guidance we should all be able to find our way.

There is a way to work with the elements in design; it is similar to the way the elements are worked with in shiatsu and acupuncture for good health and healing. In this way the elements are seen as constellations in a cycle of change, they all exist in relation to each other, and so the design process works in a dialogue with the elements. FIRE for instance, is the heart of the home, WATER is the circulation, and EARTH is the doors. Earthy shapes are well grounded and rounded, Watery shapes are flowing. There are shapes and forms and functions that relate more to one element than another, and so there is a language of design that we can use in a dialogue with the architecture and interior design of the home. Design is an aspect of this subject that will have to be saved for another book. In the meantime if you want some inspiration, try talking to others online at **www.homesouls.com**. I hope the website will grow as a meeting place and an online library and resource centre, for stories, ideas and information about home and Soul, and healthy house design.

In this book I just want to say, use your imagination to consider how your space feels, what it says, and what you think it needs, so this is what I will discuss next.

Illuminate your experience so meaning shines through in the form of what you do.

Whatever you do, make it glorious, for your acts of creation are everyday prayers.

Use your imagination

What qualities of design will best support your issues?

What atmosphere do you want to create?

What story do you want to tell?

A building takes shape through its conception as an idea, the gathering of materials, and a period of labour, to its eventual birth as a useful place. Then it is handed over by the architect and the builders to enter the service of others. Through the quality of the land and the building materials, the nature of the time, and the thoughts, feelings and activities of all those who created it, the building is invested with a story that will continue to grow with the passage of time and the people who use it. When we experience a building, not only do we see the product of someone's labour, we experience a part of their intrinsic nature invested in that place. All the people involved in making a home invest something of themselves in the process, and the story of your home grows in time as you enter another chapter of your life, to build upon what has past.

How you place yourself within your home and the things you choose to have around you are ingredients that flavour your

experience in life. You place yourself within your home by the way
you relate to it, how you choose to use it, and what you do in
certain areas, so pay attention to what you surround yourself with.

Here are some of my personal treasures. These things are
homeopathic, things I place within my home to nourish and ease
the journey of my life.

The black crystal obsidian, I
found at a beach near my home
known as Druidstone. It was all
alone in the middle of the sand
when I alone was on the beach, as
if we were destined to meet.
'Black velvet' is what the healers call it: "its subtle energies attract
the spiritual adventurers," they say. I find it really helps me with
my writing.

The clear quartz crystal, I found at my favourite place, 'Bedd
Arthur', meaning King Arthur's grave. The landscape there is full
of crystal, but this one seemed meant for me. It is an "excellent
channel of healing and good for the Soul," I am told.

I scooped the driftwood out of
a stream in a moment of contemplation. It engages my imagination. I wonder, how did it get
here? *Perhaps a little boy in conversation with his father threw it in the
water… And how did it get to them?*

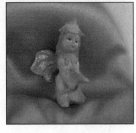

My imagination connects me to this piece
of driftwood. What a journey it has had
and what stories it has to tell. All the fine
lines rubbed away by the stream remind
me to take my time, that life is a journey
and that I should savour the delights along
the way.

The little fairy with a broken wing appeared in my office one
day. Left there by my absent-minded daughter, it captured my
attention, diverting my gaze from the computer screen to remind

me that we are all children at heart, that life should be fun and that this book should not become too serious and stuffy.

My grandmother's spoon is something we use every day to stir our tea. Its design is not appealing to me, but the memories it holds are beautiful. When I use it I think of kindness, nourishment and being of service to others. I remember how Nan loved flowers, especially roses; she used to talk to them, and although we thought it a bit odd at the time, her flowers were so beautiful and her home so filled with grace, so perhaps there was method in her madness.

The life and beauty of the flowers took on new meaning for me a few years ago, through a conversation with a follower of the anthroposophical teachings of Rudolf Steiner. She told me a delightful story: "There is purpose to the flowers' beauty," she said. "Elemental beings inhabit every flower, they long to be set free, and we can liberate them through recognition of their beauty. So if you stop to smell a rose and delight upon its fragrance and appearance, its elemental inhabitant is set free and dances about with joy." Fact or not, I love this story, and often remember it when arranging flowers within my home. To pause and appreciate the beauty of a flower is to delight in the sensual pleasure of being alive. A moment of attentiveness and recognition of beauty is a sacred experience in which we engage our senses to commune with a most beautiful aspect of divine creation.

Choosing the elements of your design is not like writing a prescription, you are not designing a cure but mixing the ingredients of your life's story to nourish you on your journey, to help you care for yourself so your Soul will be at home in your life. You may simply clean your space, get rid of some things and make it look nice. This sort of maintenance is nourishing but you can go deeper, beyond the surface of appearances to develop a healing relationship with your home and to work homeopathically with your space. To do this, consider the following qualities of design:

The Ambience: How your place feels

The Story: What your place says

The Ingredients: What the place needs

The Ambience – How your place feels

When you walk into a room you sense its atmosphere. Even with your eyes closed you can feel its ambient quality. You can sense its presence, and one room feels different to the next. The ambience of a place is the overall impression it leaves you with. It is best to feel the ambience rather than to think it, so close your eyes, be patient and wait for the impressions to come.

Consider one area or room in your home; get a sense of this space, of how you feel in this space and what you feel about it.

Now consider what this particular place means in your life. For clues perhaps take a look at the relevant scene in Chapter 2, or do a reading in Chapter 4.

Is the way it feels appropriate to the qualities that it relates to in your life?

If not, then consider how to change the way it feels.

- Now take a look around – this time seeing the details.
- How does the way it is organized make you feel?
- How does the quality of things here make you feel?
- How does the quantity of things here make you feel?
- What does it feel like to move within this space, and what does it feel like to sit within this space?
- How do the colours make you feel?
- Is there enough light?
- What about the quality of lighting?

- How does it smell to you?
- What about the temperature?
- Is it noisy? Does it need music?

Make changes that seem appropriate to you in this area of your life and home, but accept that sometimes the ambience you want cannot be practically achieved.

Take, for example, the lady whose main issue seemed to inhabit the EARTH area of her home. She saw this area as reflective of her problems with relationships, and was dismayed that this was the lavatory, cloakroom and utility room, as she did not know how to make this look good in her life.

The Orange/Yellow Runes gave her a reading for this issue: *Even the most challenging moments are a gift, so accept them graciously, looking beneath the surface wrapping and the words to find the treasure inside.*

Often you need only give the space some care and attention – cleaning, clearing and tidying is all it may need. The home reflects the way things are in our lives, sometimes we are not happy with outer appearances and we cannot see that the real beauty lives beneath the surface. So don't feel that you must get the atmosphere perfect, just do what you can do. Whatever motivates your action drives the story home. So focus your attention on the motive that moves you to do the work here. Put in the effort, because the helping hand of fate seems to favor those who are committed to their course.

The Story – What your place says

Having connected more deeply with your place is there something you would now change or remove, and what do you think the story needs?

Our secret stories are written in the details of our homes often staring us right in the face, but we do not see them. In a recent consultation I noticed on the mantle above the fireplace the figures of a mother and baby giraffe. It struck me that there was no male presence here or anywhere else in the house, and this struck a chord in me because my client, Anne, had already said to me: "*the man in my life is just not here for me*". I commented on this, and she laughed, saying, the Welsh 'Lovespoon' placed next to the mother and baby giraffe was a gift from her lover – what a perfect affirmation. A spoon is of course a symbol of nourishment. The giving of a Lovespoon is a Welsh tradition. Traditionally a lovespoon is carved from wood by a man for a woman, as a symbol of his Love or affection. Symbolically, a chain is a wish to be together forever, a diamond is for wealth or good fortune, a cross for faith, a flower for affection, and a dragon for protection (for more about lovespoons see my website www.homesouls.com).

Without giving it too much thought, Anne had placed her lover's spoon next to the mother and baby giraffe, without even realizing it, she had made a symbolic reply to her belief that "*the man in my life is just not here for me*". The fireplace was in the EARTH area of her home. Fire is the element of Love. The EARTH area of the home relates to issues about Mothering, Nourishment and Relationships. In Anne's house as in all of our homes, the life stories play themselves out, embodied in the meaning of our things.

Another client had an issue with authority – big problems with her son and her sister. We looked at the area of THUNDER because this area relates to issues of 'Authority'. On the wall were two framed pictures. One contained a poem from her sister and the other an illustration from *Winnie the Pooh* with a phrase from Christopher Robin. The problem in this area of her life was reflected in the sister's poem, it came across with anger and resentment. She decided to try to understand her sister, and to forgive her for the way she behaves. She replaced her poem with something more appropriate and focussed on Christopher Robin's positive affirmation, that said *'go on Tigger, it is easy'*, seeing this as the way forward with her son.

Often what we need is already present within our space. We just don't see it. In some places what we need is missing and in others something needs to be removed. Everything is meaningful.

Everything holds a story.

Like most people I choose my things by inspiration, there is an attraction, but at the time I might not know what the attraction is. I do know that at some time in my life, the things I choose to share my space will call for my attention, then I will consider what they mean to me and I will make a decision about how these things are placed in my life. Until then, I am not too structured about where and how I place my things in my home, I just put them where they seem to fit, where they look good to me. Time may come when you need to reposition something, remove it or bring something else into your life. If you are looking for the story, you need to look beyond the way the thing appears to be; not taking things literally but seeing them symbolically, looking beyond the frame and into the mythology. To do this you must use your memory and imagination. Perhaps you know its history, or there is something in your past that seems present in this object. Perhaps you can see yourself in it, or some other person, place or thing that is relevant in your story. Perhaps there is something mythic that captures your attention and imagination: a dragon, god or goddess, a fairy, or the freedom of a bird in flight, or maybe its general ambience invokes a feeling in you. The ability to look in this way cannot be learned from books, for what you see is personal to you. In the same way that no one else can accurately interpret your dream and no one else can know the way you are feeling, only you can know the deepest story in your things. To know something in this way you must sit with it for a while. To understand is to 'stand under'. So be with your things, let them rain their truth down upon you.

Sometimes the truth behind something is at first imperceptible, we have to give it time to unfold, and this unfolding becomes a journey where one thing leads to another, a process of discovery that happens not at once but one step at a time.

To illustrate this point I have included a story about my wife's connection with a mechanical spider in the WATER area of our home. You will come to her story soon in the section on *Learning from Experience*.

Sometimes it is not literally the thing itself but our association with it that matters. In my consultation with Anne, I was also drawn to look at the MOUNTAIN area of her home and to a cabinet in that area. At the time we were talking about what she wanted to achieve with her life. She told me the cabinet belonged to her grandfather and I asked her: *"If he were present now, what is the wisest thing he might say?"* She replied, *"He always used to say that time is the essence of a contract."* Then she realized what that meant to her in this part of her life story. She took it to mean that paying attention to the quality of the time and being present in the moment is the essence of her Sacred Contract. This to her was an important statement about her life's purpose. Her grandfather's cabinet from that moment on became her touchstone. She had turned to it for inspiration and it had become a bridge linking her story to his so that she could draw strength from his presence and his wisdom.

In another client's house a cabinet held a different story. Located in the THUNDER area, it was filled with things relating to a part of her life that was now over – but she was not over it. It was important that she dealt with the cabinet, paying attention to its place within her story, cutting ties and letting go of many of the things it contained. Through blessing and forgiveness her life would move on.

The ingredients – What your place needs

In this new age of energy medicine there are many therapeutic ingredients for design including color, crystals, aroma, and flower essences. There is so much choice, and with so much choice it is often difficult to get things started. The fear of getting it wrong holds some people back, so I implore you to be bold, and to heed the words of WH Murray from The Scottish Himalaya Expedition, 1951:

"But when I said that nothing had been done I erred in one important matter. We had definitely committed ourselves and were halfway out of our ruts. We had put down our passage money – booked a sailing to Bombay. This may sound too simple, but is great in consequence. Until

one is committed, there is hesitancy, the chance to draw back, always ineffectiveness. Concerning all acts of initiative (and creation), there is one elementary truth the ignorance of which kills countless ideas and splendid plans: that the moment one definitely commits oneself, the providence moves too. A whole stream of events issues from the decision, raising in one's favour all manner of unforeseen incidents, meetings and material assistance, which no man could have dreamt would have come his way. I learned a deep respect for one of Goethe's couplets:

'Whatever you can do or dream you can, begin it. Boldness has genius, power and magic in it!'"

Learning from experience

DIARY NOTE November 2004

As I am writing this, Jackie is about to discover what is going on in the WATER area of her life. This is so fresh we don't know where it is leading yet, but she has picked up the thread and is following it now.

The mechanical spider.
Just the other day Jackie noticed a plastic toy spider on the shelf in the WATER area of our home, put there some time ago by our little boy because it doesn't work any more – waiting for someone to sort it out. Jackie doesn't have the time or the inclination to sort it out, she spends so much time looking after the family and caring for others as a therapist and teaching women's health; things she is not inspired to do any more.

With her energy depleted she became ill, and then she noticed the spider. She has often thought of herself as a spider weaving intuition and threads of knowledge into patterns that her family, friends and clients can understand. A spider is creative and in

some cultures it is seen as the mother of the world. But this is a mechanical spider. Jackie sees herself in this spider and her actions recently had become mechanical and devoid of creative inspiration.

The spider's neighbour on the shelf is a vase filled with feathers. She has no idea how the feathers got there, but feathers are also very meaningful to her. When she was an art student her favorite work was based on feathers. Her best piece was a large sculpture which she still hopes to get cast one day, but can never justify the expense.

The wooden bowl and the little picture are also part of her story, but my point is already made: these objects reflect what is going on in Jackie's life. More specifically, they reflect what is going on in the WATER area of her life.

What she says is revealing: *"I should really be doing healing, because I am good at it and people want it from me,""I should really sort the spider out,"* and *"I should not resent my role as mother."*

But the Soul calls out to be nourished. Doing always what she "should do" and not what really inspires her drains her life-force and makes her ill. While ill she has been reading a book called: *Finding your own North Star, how to Claim the Life you were Meant to Live.* Maybe she will find what she is looking for in the book, but I know the answer lies on the shelf, with the spider and the pot of feathers. Concerns about money, lack of energy, and what one should be doing with one's life are WATER issues. Working in the WATER area will help Jackie to go with the flow.

DIARY NOTE December 2004

Spiders in the web.
Three weeks ago I wrote about Jackie's mechanical spider. We continue to be aware of its presence in the WATER area, and the issues it brings to the surface. It is this awareness that sets the wheels of change in motion. Two weeks ago Jackie went away to help teach a week-long course in Color Light Therapy. Just before her return we were cleaning the house, when my daughter

Charlotte called me into the Water area. A spider had spun a large web filled with hundreds of baby spiders.

Charlotte is scared of spiders and wanted to know whether to vacuum them up, as soon the house would be filled with grown spiders. I was delighted to see the web and the spiders, but I knew Jackie had to discover their message and determine their fate.

When she arrived home Jackie did not notice the web. What caught her attention was something I had not noticed. My son had left his skateboard on the doorstep to this area, and it was called "Spiderman". I showed her the web filled with the little spiders but the mother was absent and the nest a bit depleted. Charlotte admitted she could not bear to live with all the spiders so she had vacuumed them up.

"Last night," she said, *"I had a dream about spiders. The ones I was scared of were coming to get me and the others were walking away."* I told her the spiders represent her fears and asked if she could rid herself of fear by killing everything she is scared of? She thought then the solution might be to put the spiders' nest in the garden, but then she envisioned all the spiders coming towards the house and there would be nowhere for her to go. So the issue of fear for Charlotte had come to the surface in this area of our home. She likes to draw spiders, so I suggested she might study them for a while. Soon after, another big spider appeared in the web to replace the one she had killed. We are still living with it.

I called in a plumber to fix some long-term problems in this same area of our home. The problems were hard to fix, they took more effort, more time and cost a lot more than would normally be expected. While the plumber was working in this area I became ill. It is unusual for me to get ill, I was revisited by a chest problem I first had as a child, and then again when I took the plunge to give up architecture and work with homesouls.

As all this has been taking place in our lives we have been watching, learning and making choices. We are informed by the circumstances unfolding in our home, aware that all we see is a reflection of what we feel deep inside. The WATER element is stirring in our lives right now. The issue for Charlotte is fear. For Jackie the issues are Mothering and Creativity, as sometimes she feels she has lost herself in all the mothering. For me the issue is about my path in life, and having the faith and courage to put my homesouls work out to a much wider audience.

To continue with Jackie's story: the spiders now appear to her as a reflection of how abundant her life really is. She chose Glass Runes for a reading on their meaning. The reading confirmed what she felt deep down:

Purple/Red MOUNTAIN/FIRE
May beauty grace your life

Let beauty be born from your truth, love and passion, rising from the depths of who you truly are to become the way you experience the world and the way you express yourself in the world. Look and you will find beauty everywhere – let it grow within you, let it give you roots to ground you, let it make you light for flight, let it grow beyond you into the family, and beyond the family into the community to illuminate the far-off places.

Jackie read this and then said, "*I really love my life!*"

DIARY NOTE May 2005

Spiderman.

Almost a year and a half since the spider issues were raised. I went for a walk with my friend Ed. I had given him a copy of my manuscript to read, and I was keen to hear what he had to say about it. He asked me if I had ever seen the movie 'Spiderman', and I said yes. He said that Spiderman had issues about putting himself out there. He could not neglect his duty to do what he had been blessed to do, but in doing this, it put him in the public eye and he did not want to be so visible, that is why he wore a mask and a spider suit. I had spoken to Ed over the years about where I thought my homesouls work was going, and how inevitable it seemed that I was going to be torn between my private life in Wales, and the Calling for me to be more public with my work. Ed recognized these as Spiderman issues, and I thought he was very perceptive to see the link between me and the Spiderman skateboard that my son had left on the doorstep. He knew my concerns about making myself more visible in order to promote the homesouls work.

DIARY NOTE November 2006

Spinning and weaving.
Two years on from when Jackie discovered the mechanical spider in her life. The spider has been there in the WATER area all this time, to keep her awake to the issues, and awake to the possibilities of finding her own North Star. In June of this year when we were having a family day out at the Royal Welsh farming show Jackie fell  in love with Alpacas, and now in November the mechanical spider has been given away to a goodwill shop and Jackie has started her breeding herd. So this is where the spider has led her, to find her own North Star in the form of breeding Alpacas and spinning and weaving their fine fibre into fabrics and garments.

DIARY NOTE February 2007

The Spider gift.
I am approaching the deadline to give my manuscript to the publisher, so this will be the last diary note I make about the spider in our life. Today our good friend Helen brought Jackie a gift, a 'Silver Spider'. It is a beautiful object and Jackie has made a special

place for it on the cabinet in the FIRE area. So the last thing I write as a diary note is inspired by the spider gift, it will not be a conclusion, for there are no conclusions – as one door closes another door opens. We move with change and we gather experience along the way. Life is a never-ending story. From my point of view, the spider has made an appearance again at an opportune time, entering our lives just as I am finishing my book. I asked The Glass Runes what I should say about the spider as a final diary note. This is the reading:

Blue/White WATER/HEAVEN
Faith in your journey

Whatever your story, whatever your faith, find a way to close the gap on separation, for we all hail from the same source, we are all gifted, and we are all blessed with a life that will help us become whole.

The spider's body is like the figure of 8, symbolic of the infinite possibilities of creation, perhaps even symbolic of the eight elements. Its presence in our mythology is as the weaver, mischief-maker and storyteller; a wise fool that twists the truth and spins the yarn to send us lifelines. Spider made the first web and now we are making them – the World Wide Web reaches beyond place to connect us all in cyberspace, and as time goes on we will learn to live with much deeper and transcendent connections. Spider so often in mythology appears as the mother and the weaver of life's stories. She casts her net wide across all life, so that every person, place and thing is connected. She weaves the fabric of our lives and the garments of our habitation, and when one thing changes in her web the whole web experiences the sensation.

To my imagination she says: *Be the change you want to see in the world, spin your web and be creative with your life.*

Home as a theatre of Soul

The home of Soul is always in need of attention. An old proverb says: *When your house is finished, it is time to die.* In the home, as in life, there is always something to be done. Home is like a theatre of Soul, in which the story of life plays out, its creative direction is our role: We set the scenes and move the characters into play, we place the props and direct the performance, and what if we do not like the whole script? Then we have the authority to make some changes.

We exist in the midst of Soul, it is not the other way around – Soul is not in me, I am in Soul. The name 'homesouls' has a cosy ring to it, but let's not get too comfortable within this image. Home is where I place myself, but Soul does not belong to me. I am in my home, and perhaps my home is within me, but Soul cannot be contained, and it is not a container. All we see of Soul are images. Our connection is through the imagination; this is indeed another nation, an invisible landscape, a nation of images, reflecting the way life is. The elements and the images map themselves out in our homes, feeding us a line that we can follow, a story line that leads us through the theatre of Soul, to find our way home.

House plans can be read as blueprints of our lives, and the details of the home tell the story of what is going on in our lives. Each area of the home holds a different theme, and it is all accessible, open to view, so that we can work with it.

Once I did a consultation for a priest. We went through his house looking at the ways the different areas relate to his life and his beliefs, and at the end of the consultation he said to me, "I can see my home as a 'spiritual telephone', I call out and it calls back". He worked with his home as if in prayer. At the time he was particularly concerned about his daughter who was living away from home, so he set up an area in which he could focus on his relationship with her. He chose to do this in the EARTH area, in a corner of the room that became his direct-line to her.

We are the authors of our own life stories. We create the script, set the scene and walk the path of our own choosing. Destiny's hand deals the cards that we must play with, but how we play, and what moves we make are up to us.

If life were a game, the elements would be the cards: suits to work with for success and abundance in a game that would take us deeper. The elements are keys to understanding our living experience; they shape the territory in which our body, mind and spirit live and they provide clues for us to find ourselves and our way in life. They are archetypes that hold the whole meaning of our lives, dialoguing with each other and with each of us and all of us collectively, even when we are unaware of their existence. They help to shape our identities and give our lives the context in which we place ourselves. Yet they remain invisible and speak a silent language that works its way through the symptoms, symbols and synchronicities that animate our lives. WATER is the flow of your life. MOUNTAIN is your inner strength. THUNDER is your authority. WIND is your drive. FIRE is your truth. EARTH is your relationships. LAKE is your innocence, and HEAVEN is your boundaries. UNITY is the sacred centre, in which all the elements are together as one.

Each day through every moment of our lives we shape the story of our lives. What we think becomes our biography, and how we choose to deal with our life situations determines how happy and content we feel. Instead of reminiscing at the end of our lives, life could be so much better if we were to reflect upon our stories as they unfold, reviewing the scenes in which we play the leading role, considering the characters we choose to play and the directions we choose to take. You are the creative director of your own life story. Your mind scripts a complex role for you to play, full of mystery, tragedy, romance and conflict: making judgements about other people, places and things and bringing them into your story. Your life takes place within the context of your story, its territory is not only where you live, work and play, but also within the things that condition your life. Your adopted beliefs and the influence of others help to set the scene to become the stage on which your life plays out.

Like Dorothy in the *Wizard of Oz* and *Alice Through the Looking-*

Glass, you have embarked upon a journey that will inform your sense of belonging. Born into a world you do not understand, suffering loss, you journey on, making discoveries that will eventually lead you home. When you get there you will know so much more about yourself and your place in the world, feeling more connected with all that you have and more compassionate towards those who share your story.

The Script

UNITY

Every choice is a thread in the great fabric of life that connects all the parts to a greater whole and connects your life with the lives of everyone else. Life, it seems, moves in a continuous spiral without ending or beginning. Feeling fulfilled and becoming enlightened are just moments on the journey, through which we process our lives to become more whole. Nothing really dies, there is only transformation; all things have their time and then return to their source. The Tao of life cannot be explained any concept we have just falls short, because we understand our existence in fragments and we each construct our view in different ways, never seeing the whole picture.

WATER

Water connects you to your source and carries your life on its journey. Being in the flow, racing against the clock, taking your time, having faith, fearing what will happen next, and believing that you cannot afford it. All of these are WATER scripts. We take them all onboard as we navigate our way on the journey of life.

MOUNTAIN

Mountain is a pause: a threshold of silence, a moment for contemplation, adjustment and centring – to pause and take a breath, and then to breathe new life into what will become.

THUNDER

Thunder is the Script and you are the Author. Fate delivers the people, places and things, and you script them into your story. You decide what role they will play in your life, and how they will influence you. Becoming self-conscious, you begin to see yourself as a product of your situation, you look outside to find happiness in other places and other things, seeking approval and love from others. Your circumstances influence the choices you make and condition the person you will become. You adopt a role in life and wear the masks to suit the script. First they call it growing up, then they call it fitting in. The adult encourages the child to be clever, to learn the skills to control its world. Innocence is something the adult grows out of, and grows up from.

WIND

Wind is the force behind your ego, the motivator of change and the creative director of your whole life story. In a quest for survival you jump into the driving seat, taking your place in the human race, riding the winds of change, finding plenty to experience and plenty to do, meeting temptation and desire along the way, sometimes going by the main road and sometimes by the sidetracks. WIND drives your career and your financial acumen. It is your sex drive and your lust for life. Our feet may hardly touch the ground as one climbs the ladders of success and personal stairways to Heaven, racing against the clock, finding there is so much to do and so little time to do it in. As the ego dominates, life becomes a competitive struggle; we gain, we achieve, we possess, and the price we pay is freedom, for then we must protect and defend what we call our own. We stake our claims and defend our right to have and to hold what we desire, and to be individual. In the race we may lose our sense of belonging, thinking the grass is always greener on the other side, and longing for approval.

FIRE

Fire is Realisation – a wake-up call – a sense that there is more to life, that something special is missing. You may ask yourself: Where is love? Where is truth? And where is my sense of belonging? Soul alerts you to your attachments and addictions, to where you are sending your attention and your energy; to how you invest your power and spend your time. You call your Spirit back from missions that do not serve your truth, your love and your sense of well-being.

EARTH

Earth is sharing – a call to open your hands, mind and heart, and to expand your boundaries through sharing and giving, an invitation to inhabit a richer place. Sharing is a creative act that calls you to be open and receptive to others. The closed hand of possession makes one protective, guarding against loss. The hand that has taken now opens to give and receive and you enter a union of belonging with others. To show devotion, to be of service and to give of oneself are liberating acts of kindness that loosen the ego's grip.

LAKE

Lake is the inner landscape of your deeper self, and you are its seeker, realizing that love for others is incomplete without self-love, and a peaceful world is incomplete without inner peace. Happiness in the company of others does not fulfill one's whole being; there are hidden depths to one's life that must be explored. This is a spiritual quest to know more about oneself and one's place in the divine plan of life: exploring spirituality, questioning reality, piercing the veil of illusions, and discovering other dimensions to life. The Ego becomes defensive; realising its loss of control it questions your judgement and even your sanity.

HEAVEN

Heaven helps you to see clearly: to discover your Heaven on Earth. The veneers of illusion peel away and you are no longer fooled by the way things appear to be. Enlightenment marks the death of ego: no more judgements, no more attachments, no more striving, nor seeking perfection. Letting go of all these things, you arrive back home to know your place as if for the first time.

The Scene

Life takes place somewhere. Our five senses give us the experience of where that is, but they do not perceive the invisible landscape that sets the scene in which our lives take place. The invisible landscape has no borders or boundaries, it exists in a dimension beyond what we see, hear, touch, taste and smell. Without form it cannot be perceived through any of the common senses, yet intuitively we know it is there, because we go there when we sleep, we go there for inspiration and to collect our thoughts. We are always there: Soul inhabitants of space, members of a collective without frontiers or conventions, at home in a landscape beyond the mirror of our visible lives. The landscape itself cannot be seen but its elements are part of our everyday experience, undercurrents to the things that happen in our lives.

UNITY

Here you are at the center of everything in your life, at the center of the wheel around which all the elements of your experience and your story revolve. You dwell here on the threshold between the seen and the unseen, all the things you desire, envision and fear are out there at the edge on the horizon waiting for an invitation to enter your scene. Whatever you reach for is there like a beacon to illuminate your journey. Whenever you are lost, lonely or discontent, something will appear on your horizon, prompting you to make your next move. Our eyes meet at the same horizon, it is the level plane from which we all draw our perspectives, construct our reality and clothe ourselves in the facts and theories that offer the comfort we are looking for. Some people set their sights high, others lower, we each have a personal view of the horizon that puts us in our place. So we journey towards it, sometimes thinking we are above or below the line, sometimes taking our elevation and position to seriously, but as we move and change and grow the horizon moves with us. We look to close the gap, longing for what is missing, or for what we cannot see, but the horizon is always distant, and yet always relative to ones particular point of view.

Enter WATER

Everyone and everything in your life is connected, the course for your life is set, and you must find the way to go with its flow; greeting life as a meeting of circumstances that serve your journey to become more whole.

Enter MOUNTAIN

The gateway between your outer and inner kingdoms. The Sanctuary of your innocence – the quiet place at the core of who you are. This is where you hold your centre knowing you are safe, because no one else can enter this place; no one can influence the essence of who you truly are.

Enter THUNDER

The awakening force; setting the scene for you to leave your silent inner world of being for the outer active world of doing, to enter your life experience with the authority to do something in the world.

Enter WIND

The moving force, bringing abundance and opportunity, and setting the scene for you to become the pioneer in your own life story.

Enter FIRE

It lights your way, to mark the edge of what has been and what has yet to come, illuminating the horizon for you to see the road ahead more clearly. It is your sunshine and your fuel; giving warmth for Love, heat for passion and light for Truth.

Enter EARTH

For you must become the sovereign of your abundant and fruitful life: to treat it tenderly, and govern it justly, nourishing all that enter your dominion.

Enter LAKE

To find the place of magic and mystery in your life, to discover yourself as a child hiding in the shadows; to let the light in, and unlock the doors to your deeper and darker secrets. It is autumn in your life, a time to remove the masks and shed the skins that no longer fit the person you truly are.

Enter HEAVEN

To choose your own reality, and find your own way home. From here there are many roads you may take, they all lead ultimately to the same place: you may follow your own Will or take the path of life's calling – the choice is yours. Deconstruct your world of appearances, to see more clearly and choose the best way home.

The Cast

The homesouls journey is a process through which you find contentment in being who you truly are and accepting your place in the world. You are cast into life as a Pilgrim (WATER), to take part in the Divine act of creation, to know who you truly are (MOUNTAIN), and to make a difference in the world. You are the Author (THUNDER), the Creative Director (WIND), the Star (FIRE), the Co-star (EARTH), the Genius (LAKE), and the Editor (HEAVEN).

These are eight aspects of who you truly are: archetypal elements of a subplot that underlies living reality.

UNITY

From the viewpoint of Soul we are eternally children, always at the beginning of our journey. Our point of reference will always be where we are right now. We need look no further than where we are right now. Those who begin to fathom the unfathomable believe they find its hidden dimensions. But it is no place. There is no 'thing' really there, all they find are maps, methods and clues that help the seeker become the seer. By all means look, for what you see is your projection. If something needs to change, simply change your view then your experience will change too.

In the words of Pierre Pradervand:

"Deep inside you exists a space of infinite beauty and rest, of total uncon-ditional love, a space of goodness without bounds, of unshakeable peace and calm, of dancing joy and playful being, of limitless vision and infinite abundance…

This space constitutes our true being. No event in life, no crippling disease, torment nor suffering, no childhood trauma, absolutely nothing will ever mar its wholeness, which constitutes our true identity."

In WATER

You are a pilgrim cast into life's story to journey through the school of life. Majoring in your vision quest, to know yourself, explore your potential, and find your own way home.

At birth you leave your place of comfort and belonging to journey into unknown waters, to navigate life's ebbs and flows following a distant voice that calls for your return, "Come home again, come home again!" it calls through the annals of time. Sometimes you will wait too long, not acting when the time is right; sometimes you will move too fast, driven by impatience and ambition; always you will learn from your experience. Each failure is simply a rehearsal, another chance will come, and you will learn to make sweet honey from your old failures.

Life is a dance between pleasure and pain – sometimes a comedy and sometimes a tragedy. The Pilgrim may grow old and weary, finding excuses not to see the lighter side of life, but the spirit will always be young and innocent with time to dance.

In MOUNTAIN
The Pilgrim meets the Prophet at the Mountain, and from this peak of your potential you descend into life, having accepted Soul contracts to do what must be done. Here you are in-tuition – your higher self can coach you to know your innocence and your potential, and to follow your intuition on a journey into the valleys of life.

In THUNDER
Here you awaken to your vision of the world. You are the author of your own life story. You gather ideas about what you might do and become and set your mind on action. The choices you make affect the lives of others so you must learn to see the bigger picture and use your influence well.

In WIND
Here the ego takes control, for the ego loves a drama. You are the creative director orchestrating the action in your life. You rise to the challenges of your life's direction to go places and get things done. Your ego is always at the centre of the action, trying to present an inflated picture of your own self-importance.

In FIRE

You are the Star of your life story, your ego wants recognition and appreciation, it wants to feel special so it takes care of your image and looks for the spotlight. Your Spirit shines most brightly when not eclipsed by ego, it helps you to see yourself in your true light and to illuminate the lives of others. You are brilliant, so shine your light unto the world.

In EARTH

Here you recognise everyone else as a Star and realise we all co-star in one another's stories. Without relationship there would be no drama. The ego loves the drama – the spirit loves authenticity.

In LAKE

You are pure Genius at play within your story, stripping away the illusions, receiving inspiration as your gift, and finding the hidden joy.

In HEAVEN

You are the Editor. Your spirit knows the whole story; it holds the keys to your enlightenment. The ego is a nitpicker and a critical judge, placing importance on things that don't really matter.

The Way

Frequently we come to crossroads in our lives and have to choose between this and that, deciding which direction to take. Ultimately all roads lead back to the centre, but there are main roads and there are sidetracks. When you go with the flow of your life, allowing your deeper self to guide your way, providence is at your side, lending its helping hand to relieve unnecessary burdens. This doesn't mean life is easy this way, but that on your true path the obstacles and problems you encounter are the ones that are meant for you. The sidetracks are the ego's choice: thinking the grass is always greener somewhere else, and searching for those pastures, it takes you the long way home. The main road is Destiny's favored path: on the main road everything comes your way.

UNITY
There is stillness at the centre, but often we do not feel this. Frequently we lose our centre, getting caught up in the motion of the wheel, going off at tangents, heading somewhere. We head off into the elements, off into the journey of life, for there are things we need to experience and things we need to learn.

With WATER
The main road is the way of acceptance and surrender, going with the flow to reach your highest potential. Becoming sidetracked, you try too hard, pushing when you should pull and moving when you should rest. Through fear you resist the flow, and when you are not present in each moment, you miss life's beauty and its magic.

With MOUNTAIN
The main road is the way of compassion and contentment that leads to a state of tranquillity, a place where you perceive your own reality and come to know yourself and to love yourself, content to be who you are. Becoming sidetracked, you get bogged down, defining truth in self-serving ways, becoming manipulative or stubborn and immovable.

With THUNDER

The main road is the way of forgiveness and blessing. With faith in your divine and inner guidance, you move on, blessing all you meet along the way, developing immunity to the negative influences of others, and forgiving those who treat you badly. Often forgiveness is necessary before we can move on. Becoming sidetracked, you get jealous, angry and resentful, lacking hope and trust, and being unable to forgive.

With WIND

The main road is the way of honor. On this road you maintain your integrity whilst pursuing opportunities and resisting temptations that break your personal code of honour. Sidetracked, you become lost, dissatisfied, addicted, and you take advantage of others, lacking commitment to your own creative direction.

With FIRE

The main road is the way of self-realization. It guides you to make choices that reflect who you truly are, channelling your energy only into things you believe in, and being true to your word. Becoming sidetracked, you focus upon your own self-image, self-expression, and desire to be seen and heard, consuming too much, and channelling your energy in ways that do not serve your life's true purpose.

With EARTH

The main road guides you to have compassion for everyone and to honor yourself and others as part of a holy union. You come to understand your relationships as sacred agreements along a sacred path leading to unconditional love. Sidetracked, life becomes heavily burdened with worries and concerns that do not nourish your life.

With LAKE

The main road helps you explore creation and live a meaningful life guided by Spirit, following your intuition with a sense that you belong within your own biography, biology, and living environment. On the main road you discover your creativity to transcend the mundane, to love unconditionally, let go of attachments and no longer need other people's approval. Becoming sidetracked leads to feelings of shame, lack of personal identity, the need for approval, narcissistic behaviour, denial of spirit, and fear of the unknown.

With HEAVEN

On the main road you are ordained into the service of humanity: surrendering personal will to Divine Will, following your life's calling and your Divine guidance to be creative in your own unique way. Becoming sidetracked, you take the long way home, dealing with problems and burdens you don't need to bear. Having too much control over relationships and events will lead you this way, as will enslaving yourself to demands that do not serve your calling.

On this homesouls journey you take responsibility for what is happening in your life – taking the wheel and setting the course to explore your life and your home, to find some answers and to make some changes.

If imagination is the landscape of Soul, then Soul is at home in a story. We build our lives on Story. In a sense we dream our world into existence, everything starts with an idea, it has an image, we build upon our images, and they become our experience. Everything we know and everything we do starts in life as fantasy ideas that we build upon. We construct realities from figments of our imagination.

I have chosen to present this subject to you as a story, and to take you on a journey to look at your home as a stage upon which the story of your life plays out. Perhaps it is because I find facts so dry, and I feel more at home in a story. But if it is a story, then how can it be true? You might well ask.

The search for truth is a personal journey for which there are many vehicles. Each one of us must choose our suitable vehicle.

Just because we have faith in our choice, and it gets us where we want to go, does not mean it is true for someone else.

There is danger in climbing too high, when we make our truth too literal. "True Feng Shui" and "Authentic Feng Shui" are banners under which some consultants practice. If there is something sacred about Soul, it is not, in my view, to be defined as 'truth', as if a pot of gold, into which the worthy and the enlightened stake their claim.

Nor should the readings at the end of this book be taken too literally. There is much more to know than what has been said. As you work with them, the meaning of the elements, and your familiarity with their relationships will grow beyond what I have stated in the readings.

These things are said: "*Follow your true path*", "*look for truth beyond appearances*", "*become who you truly are*", "*be in touch with your true nature*".

So what is truth for me? In my book, the search for 'truth' is the journey into Soul, if 'truth' were a pot of gold, it is to the rainbow that we should turn, not to profit from what is at the end, but to color our lives with its beauty.

Chapter 4

homesouls® Oracle Readings

READINGS INDEX

Purple/Yellow	Mountain/Earth	Sovereign rock – Empowering through devotion 215
Purple/Turquoise	Mountain/Lake	Initiation 216
Purple/White	Mountain/Heaven	Service through wisdom 217
Purple/Blue	Mountain/Water	Guiding wisdom 217

GREEN

Green/Clear	Thunder/Unity	Your creation story 219
Green/Green	Thunder/Thunder	The wake-up call 220
Green/Orange	Thunder/Wind	Living with your story 221
Green/Red	Thunder/Fire	Authenticity 222
Green/Yellow	Thunder/Earth	Everyday hero 223
Green/Turquoise	Thunder/Lake	Influential behaviour 224
Green/White	Thunder/Heaven	Management of power 225
Green/Blue	Thunder/Water	Moving on 226
Green/Purple	Thunder/Mountain	Small is beautiful 226

ORANGE

Orange/Clear	Wind/Unity	Yield and overcome 228
Orange/Orange	Wind/Wind	Creative direction 228
Orange/Red	Wind/Fire	Harmony in the family 229
Orange/Yellow	Wind/Earth	Creative thinking 230
Orange/Turquoise	Wind/Lake	Inner truth 231
Orange/White	Wind/Heaven	Empowering reserve 231
Orange/Blue	Wind/Water	The way of energy 232
Orange/Purple	Wind/Mountain	Centering 233
Orange/Green	Wind/Thunder	Achieving what is meant to be 234

RED

Red/Clear	Fire/Unity	Let there be light 236
Red/Red	Fire/Fire	The tears of a clown 237
Red/Yellow	Fire/Earth	Forward in abundance 237
Red/Turquoise	Fire/Lake	Meeting opposition 238
Red/White	Fire/Heaven	Sharing your light 239
Red/Blue	Fire/Water	Prepare for change 240
Red/Purple	Fire/Mountain	Longing 241

YELLOW

TURQUOISE

WHITE

Clear/Clear   *Unity/Unity*
Contentment

We live in longing to find belonging.
A heartfelt calling of the Soul
To find our way home
To know contentment

Then all is well and there is nothing to be done.

Clear/Blue   *Unity/Water*
Just being

A great warrior makes peace.
When hearts are at peace no one needs a healer.
A great healer wants to be redundant.
In stillness the warrior has no mind for war.
Through stillness the healing channels open.
Surrender and be still.

Clear/Purple   *Unity/Mountain*
To Know One's Place in the Human Race

Know the value of what you think, say and do.
Think just enough.
Say just enough.
Do just enough.
Those who race ahead complete their journey before their time, they win their race but lose so much along their way.
Economy of time and energy.
It is economic to pay attention to each moment, for those who know the true value of their time can be generous with their attentions.
Mercy. The merciful are courageous, brave enough to shun the prizes and the glory, fair and forgiving even when they have been badly treated. It takes courage to show compassion when others

would seek revenge.

Humility. It is better to know one's place of value in this world than to make claims without foundation.

Place the qualities of economy, mercy and humility at the center of who you are. When one is at home with mercy, economy and humility, others come to call to know their courage, generosity and leadership.

Clear/Green *Unity/Thunder*
Awakening to the Illusions that Shape Your World

You are the author of your own life's story.

Know that in this world of appearances the way of changes works through paradox; things are not the way they appear to be.

What you search hardest for is closest to you, the faults you find in others are things you dislike about yourself, and in your problems you will find your greatest opportunities.

Clear/Orange *Unity/Wind*
Life Is Your Present

Ordinary life is an everyday prayer.
Be at home in your place of enchantment.
Longing for your future you pass your present by.
You can chase your future
but you will never catch it.
You can shape your future
but it will never look the way you imagined.
You can fill your life with things to do,
but things will never fulfil you.
The winds of change blow towards you –
you cannot out run them.
They blow towards you bearing gifts –
Life is your present.

Clear/Red   *Unity/Fire*
Calling Your Spirit Home

You invest your Spirit in what you think, say, and do.

It guides energy into your life, and illuminates the images, signs and symptoms of your body, mind and home, awakening your heart to the calling of your Soul.

Spirit is your pilot light: it warns of impending danger, ignites your creativity, manages your energy and empowers you to be brilliant.

In you it is at home.

Think only Love.

Speak only Truth.

And do the work you are called to do.

Clear/Yellow   *Unity/Earth*
The Open Hand

Know the way of energy.

To open is the key.

With an open mind and open heart; open your hand,
and know the way of the warrior and the way of the healer.

Take care with an open hand.

And on your way find guidance in the sign of an open hand:
Take from the hand that offers and fill the hand that needs.

Meet others with an open hand.

Extend a hand of greeting and give a hand to help, place it where it's needed and feel the joy it brings.

The open hand is welcome, so yield and let life flow.

Clear/Turquoise   *Unity/Lake*
Creation – Let it Flow and Let it Go

In the depths of innocence are all life's mysteries:
To breathe into them is to inspire oneself.
To breathe out from them is to inspire others.

A great idea takes your breath away, a great obsession takes your life away,

So be open and receptive, abundantly creative.

Breathe through your ideas, images and dreams, to let them flow and then let go – Return to innocence.

Clear/White   *Unity/Heaven*
Holistic Healing

Faith and courage know that pain and suffering are wounds that need attention, we find them on the road to enlightenment.

We are all wounded healers, alchemists with a story to tell, nursing wounds that we must enter before our lives can change.

Compassion greets pain and suffering on the road towards wholeness.

It works its alchemy and then moves on. If one person becomes attached to the suffering of another then two people are suffering.

There must be warmth in this detachment, for through cold detachment one becomes judge, jury and executioner; seeking vengeance or retribution to satisfy pain.

The world is a reflection of who you are.

You must be the change you wish to see in the world.

Heal yourself and the world heals with you.

Blue/Clear   Water/Unity
In Touch with Your True Nature

Know that all is one and let it be,
therein lies tranquillity of being.
Please the Soul through sensual pleasure,
Enjoying life's moments as your present.
Close the eyes and quiet the mind,
For the essence you seek,
Although unseen and never heard,
Is always there in your present.
What you seek will come when you know this way.

Blue/Blue   Water/Water
Journey Toward Wholeness

"Cross the great water".

These Runes call you on a journey toward wholeness.

What is the point? This question will meet you many times at your wits' end, where you come to a precipice and need to make a choice. Is this the point at which you give up or is it simply a new challenge?

In the circle of life we move beyond the center on a pilgrimage through unfamiliar landscapes in which there are many dimensions.

On this journey we make choices about direction. The heart, mind, body, may choose to go back, to find something lost or left behind to find recovery in the past. They may choose to go forward, for something is calling or driving them that way. The choice may be for the left or right, to descend into darkness or ascend towards the light.

Follow your Calling. Come home Soul, back to the center where all is one and you are content. Make the journey joyfully, make light of all that happens in your life, for light brings warmth, illumination, clarity and enlightenment.

Crossing the great water requires a pioneering spirit to be true to yourself under all conditions and to be courageous in greeting the challenges along your way.

We all come to the edge at some time. Some people are ahead of others and some parts of you are ahead of other parts. At this point of your journey it is time to pull yourself together, to look at yourself as a whole, to take care of the parts of your body and your story that are holding you back, because they need your attention as well.

To become more whole you must visit the places where your life seems restricted, damaged or empty.

You will always have enough time to do what must be done. You may think that what you need is over the hill and far away, but it is not, it is always where you are right now. You may not see it because your perspective shades your point of view and the baggage you carry requires so much of your attention. So take your time to lighten your load.

Bless yourself with the serenity to accept the things you cannot change, the courage to change the things you can, and the wisdom to know the difference.

Blue/Purple   Water/Mountain
Rising Above the Problem

This is a test on your journey through life. Its image is stretched out before you as a great expanse of water and a high mountain. Your journey must not end here so you must decide how you will continue with such obstacles in your way.

These Runes call you to realise that the obstacles in your way are there for a reason. They ask the question: are you in tune with the nature of your life?

Do you know the best way to behave when confronted with this adversity?

First it is necessary to pause and review the situation. Try to see things clearly and have the courage not to swerve from the inner laws of your being. Do what must be done to stay on your true path.

You will not rise to the challenge by assuming the role of victim or looking to apportion blame for a problem that you have actually called into your own life. And someone else cannot solve or heal the problem for you, although it may be wise to get some help.

Will you yield to the problem, finding the path of least resistance, or does this occasion in your life require that you meet it head on, cutting a straight path to it and over it?

The occasion calls to question how much trust, faith and courage you have, and how well you know yourself and your path in life. It questions your wisdom by making you choose between a brave or foolhardy action.

Blue/Green   Water/Thunder
Growing Pains

Thunder is the vision to glimpse what is on your horizon and the power to get there. Water carries you there in good time.

These Runes call you to know that times of growth are beset with difficulties at the beginning, so manage your power along the path of least resistance, being patient, whilst preparing the ground for your own deliverance.

Pause to get a sense of where you are, to see your place in the bigger scheme of things. Life has prepared you to be in this position now. Where you go from here is up to you.

Your true path is the main road that follows Destiny's calling. The sidetracks are deviations you take when frustration and impatience take hold of you.

You are the author of your own life story, but you do not control your Destiny. In partnership with the Divine you co-create your life.

When you go with the flow you move in the direction of your destiny.

There is always help at hand, but you must learn to read the signs and listen to life's Calling. *The homesouls Oracle* is a guide to help you pay attention to the signs.

Without clear vision and with so many possibilities and paths off in tempting directions, it is difficult to know which way to turn. Don't proceed until you are clear that you are on the right track.

Prepare yourself for what is to come: take time out to simplify your life, let go of all that is not meant to be, clear out the clutter, get rid of unnecessary baggage, and bring clarity to your mind. Move only when you feel the time and the conditions are right.

You cannot accelerate your development. When you force the pace you lose out on things along the way, then at a later date you must recover what you have lost.

You won't always get it right; learning from mistakes is part of growing and perfecting your way to contribute to the world.

Blue/Orange　　　　　*Water/Wind*
Nourishing Your Vision Quest

Wind and Water (Feng Shui).

To know your home as a vessel for life's journey.

Wind moves and Water flows, drawing nourishment from the deep.

Water carries the vessel and Wind fills the sails to move you on your way.

Water fills the well and Wind turns the wheel, drawing nourishment from its depths.

These Runes call you to be the pioneer in your own life story. There are things that only you must do, so nourish your vision and go your own way. Don't be tied to social conventions and other people's expectations. Un-attach: cut the ties that hold you back and do not serve your vision, for you are unique and no one else can know your way. Go with your flow and other people will follow your lead.

Drawing abundance from the inexhaustible well-spring of life, some are content to skim the surface; you must drink from the depths. Enjoy the things of the world but journey deeper.

All things come to pass in the blink of an eye. To experience life fully open your eyes wide and never be too busy to live life to the full.

It is better to experience much and say little, than to experience a little and say a lot.

The world as it appears to your eyes is but a reflection of your inner world.

Journey deeper.

Blue/Red   Water/Fire
Release

Fire and Water together cannot remain in a state of equilibrium. They are complementary but also opposites.

When Water is above, its nature is to fall. When Fire is below, its nature is to rise. Falling Water dowses Fire, and rising flames dry up Water.

This state of equilibrium is a transition point for change.

It can be a time of climax before a new beginning.

These Runes call you to make the most of this time, to bring old things to completion, to attend to the details and rejoice in what has passed, then with clear sight, to enter the next stage in your evolution.

When the light of Fire is fading at this time, do not fear the darkness because Water is there to support you and carry you through. You must have faith in what is to come next.

The dowsing effect of Water causes flames to flicker – an image of dancing light sparkling and crackling with flames fighting back, raging against the dying of the light.

Creating the ambience for joyful celebration of what is passing and what is to come.

It is important not to stay too long at the party. Retire when the work is done, and when entering the darkness of this next stage do not fear the dying of the light. Try not to grieve over what is passing, there is now cause for celebration in anticipation of what is to come, because each new dawn brings new light and new clarity.

Clarity must precede effort, so learn from what has passed.

The next chapter in your life's story is built upon the last, so bless all the circumstances that got you to this place and accept the hand of fate that will lead you on again.

Blue/Yellow   *Water/Earth*
Being an Anchor in a Community

Water becomes streams, and joins rivers that join the ocean. Earth holds Water so it may complete its journey.

These Runes call you to know your role within your community and to learn how to manage your responsibility with honour and dignity.

Individuals with separate paths and personal lives come together and are linked by their common interests.

Your role is to be an anchor to serve a community of interest. Each person is vital as a link to all the others, but your anchor is the one that holds them together. This requires greatness of spirit, consistency and strength.

You will best serve the people around you by cultivating your own character. Although they must rely on you, your position is equal to theirs – in them you will find the complement of your own nature.

So your personal development is linked with those who are drawn to this union, and each one holds a key to the development of the others.

Hold to your course every moment, because you follow a turbulent path with channels running off in tempting directions.

You must be true to your higher nature. So when you are visited by ambitious desires for position or envy towards others, you must put these feelings in their place.

Open your eyes to see the superior potential in others. Set aside judgements. Allow others to be who they are, so they may find their own way.

Blue/Turquoise   *Water/Lake*
Know your Limits

The Water element carries the life-force (*Ki*) energy that gives your life longevity, vitality and health.

You have plenty of energy to do the things that really matter, but not to waste on soulless ventures and saying things that are hurtful, meaningless and untrue. A Lake cannot hold Water without its banks. Without good boundaries we struggle to develop a good sense of who we are and how to place ourselves in the world. Work within your limitations to set your spirit free to do what must be done.

These Runes call you to ask yourself who you truly are and to live the life that is truly yours. Why do you do too much? Why do you say the things you say? What need in you are you trying to satisfy? Where do you look for approval? What are you trying to prove?

Know your place and respect other people's boundaries, taking care not to intrude in matters that are not your business.

Work with the nature of the time. Sometimes opportunities are open to you and other times they are closed.

Go with the flow – don't push against boundaries, look for the opening.

To some extent, we are prisoners of our own expectations and those of family and friends; we cannot find freedom in the rules and values others live by. We must be self-regulating and respectful, creating our own good boundaries whilst taking care that the limitations we impose are not unduly hurtful to others. Don't struggle with your difficulties with limitations. It is the seeking process that is most important, not what you will eventually find.

In seeking the truth you battle with your ego. As you loosen its grip on your life it will look to strike back, diverting your attention, encouraging you to race through the process and skip steps along the way.

When you find that you are defining truth in self-serving ways and inflating your sense of self-importance it is time to journey deeper, for the ego has the upper hand.

Blue/White   *Water/Heaven*
Faith in your Journey

Heaven calls you and Water carries you closer to the source. Enjoy the journey.

These Runes call you to know your part in the bigger picture, and see your life as an everyday prayer calling through the details of your body, home and story.

We are larger than our lives, greater than the body, more than what we see and experience. For we flow within the source and the source flows within us.

Crossing the great waters of life we can find love, light and joy, even through loss, separation and pain. We condition our lives through the way we relate to what we meet along the way. The more we lose faith and try to control what is going on, the greater loss, separation and pain we feel.

Every encounter is a Divine gift and a blessing, but often we refuse to accept the packages our gifts come in, so we close our eyes to them or turn them away. Often what we need most in life comes in the strangest packages. There is always humor in the present, perhaps a touch of irony or tragic comedy, but always a lighter side.

We are called to make light of our situations and then to journey deeper, for beyond the world of appearances there is a magical kingdom, the kingdom of all Souls and all blessings from which we are all gifted.

Whatever your story, whatever your faith, find a way to close the gap on separation, for we all hail from the same source, we are all gifted, and we are all blessed with a life that will help us become whole.

Along the way, pay attention to the details, for our calling animates our life. Taking shape in our body, home and story, it shapes the elements in our lives and weaves its way through our stories.

Look closely and you will see your life reflected in the details that surround you. They call you to recognise who you are and what you are doing and to see yourself in the bigger picture. Like clues on a treasure hunt they take you closer to what you need to know and what you need to find.

Have the patience to pay attention to the details of your life, for you will find all you need in the present – what you do with the present is up to you.

Soul longs for you to find your truth and follow its path.

Purple/Clear   *Mountain/Unity*
Belonging

To know oneself in the unity of all things
To see oneself in the image of all things
To be at home in one's form and in the form of all things
All things are united by their essence; that which cannot be explained nor seen nor touched.

With faith in the unity of all things one can know and experience the essence of creation that some call *Tao* and others call God.

Purple/Purple   Mountains
Tranquillity of Being

The place of Mountains – to reach their heights in your life is to achieve tranquillity of being. Mountains yield to the forces of nature, changing shape in time but constant in their essence.

These Runes call you to find tranquillity in your life: a natural state of inner composure, a place of peace and quiet, contentment through belonging in the moment and being at home with oneself.

One arrives at this place through a quiet heart and mind. Sometimes it is hard to find this quiet place within oneself, so go there often and get to know it well: then when you are lost it will call you home.

Practice taking time out to be with yourself and whatever happens in the moment. Know the heights that you may climb, and keep your thoughts to the immediate situation.

Know there are times for action and times for contemplation. In times of action remember to pause for the heart and mind to be quiet.

Through tranquillity one may return to innocence to see things intuitively as they really are.

Yield and you will overcome.

Tranquillity is lost through battles of the heart and mind and through battles between people.

Life free of battles is without victors and without victims. There is no need to conquer, for providence moves with you when the time is right and the way is clear.

Purple/Green   Mountain/Thunder
Nourishment

Thunder in the Mountain sweeping clean the deepest stratum of your being.

These Runes call you to pay attention to the provision of nourishment in your life: are you fulfilling your individual needs? Are you open to receive nourishment? How well do you provide for others?

We are nourished by our spirituality, diet, creativity, sexuality, exercise, rest, education, and social activities. All of this is governed by an attitude of mind, for as authors of our own life stories we are continuously reinventing ourselves.

What we choose to do for re-creation is important. The sacred vessels that we call our nature, body and home require maintenance and renewal from time to time to make room for health, abundance and Divine inspiration.

The provision of nourishment is a balance between what we take of life and what we give back.

We are all fitted by nature and Destiny to achieve certain things in life, so it is wrong to make judgements about worthiness and to look with envy or discontent at those perceived to be better off. Contribute what you can, knowing your place and your way of being in the world, and having respect and consideration for others who are different.

To give your blessings and forgiveness is a healthy form of nourishment.

At times when you are without the energy or resources to give much back, turn your attention to your own needs and to your recovery. Ask for help, for you must always be open to receive.

You will find nourishment through tranquillity of being, and others will find comfort in your tranquillity.

No matter how humble your circumstances, you should never underestimate your influence. Another person may simply be moved by your presence, and a passing statement or seemingly insignificant action may have a profound effect upon them. With the correct attitude towards life we will always receive what we need.

Purple/Orange   Mountain/Wind
Work on What has been Spoiled

The Wind cannot penetrate the Mountain, but the Mountain penetrates the Wind. Wind will bring energetic transformation, but only after contemplation.

These Runes call you to be the change you want to see in the world.

In every society, group and family there are many shared attitudes and beliefs that do not serve the common good, yet they prosper and grow. Through culture, habit and family ties, we become accustomed to inappropriate modes of behaviour. Through ignorance, blind acceptance and denial, these aspects of who we are become deeply embedded wounds, passing from one generation to the next, cutting right across the landscape of our lives to create the context in which we all struggle for survival.

When you look at the condition of the world, what you see is a part of who you are. So perform your alchemy upon yourself. Find the origin of your wounds, find what is gross and base in your attitudes and behaviour, heal yourself and transform your life. Your healing will become part of our common condition, alleviating the pain and suffering we all share.

Heed these instructions for the alchemist's brew:

"Learn through contemplation, stir up to remove stagnation, then strengthen and tranquillise so the end will be followed by a new beginning."

Take your own medicine – replace inertia and indifference with the decisiveness and energy to welcome a new age.

Purple/Red   *Mountain/Fire*
May Beauty Grace your Life

These Runes call you to pay attention to how you fashion your life, into what you direct your energy, and to whom and what you make your allegiances.

You have been fashioned in the image of the Divine – you are Divine. Let your image speak your truth and may your pleasure come from the primal depths of your nature to make you high on the experience of living. Free from the entrapments of shallow experience, your life may be filled with grace; and your experience divinely orgasmic.

Love the way you look, wearing your image as an expression of who you truly are. Illuminate your life so that beauty shines through the things you say and do.

Take your love to the highest places, getting high on beauty and sensual pleasure, but know there is still much further to go.

Beyond the realm of pleasure and pain, experience becomes Divine, transcending material form and earthly boundary.

Vanity choreographs your life to create a show for admiration, enjoying the surface, not the depths, concealing more than it shows to make you feel high on the illusion. Vanity meets you at the base camp, it pampers your whims and desires, flattering and polishing up your act.

Transcend your vanity to find true beauty.

To climb that high you must be lighter, leaving the baggage of prejudice, convention, and false impression behind.

Grace will meet you at this high place where beauty is the manifestation of Love. Grace will help you to be in love with living.

Its virtue grows through looking. Look and you will find it in a grain of sand and in a simple wildflower. Cleave the wood, lift up the stone and you will find it there.

Let beauty be born from your truth, love and passion, rising from the depths of who you truly are to become the way you experience the world and the way you express yourself in the world.

Look and you will find beauty everywhere – let it grow within you, let it give you roots to ground you, let it make you light for flight, let it grow beyond you into the family, and beyond the family into the community to illuminate the far-off places.

Purple/Yellow   Mountain/Earth
Sovereign Rock – Empowering through Devotion

Mountain becomes great by virtue of the Earth – for a rock that stands tall and great must have broad and firm foundations. Through devotion we become sovereign over the landscape of our lives, and with devotion we become a touchstone for others.

These Runes call you to achieve greatness through devotion: to be who you are without distraction, and to touch the lives of others simply by being who you are and being there for them. Through taking care, giving generously and being just, build your foundations strong so you may stand broad and straight, not proud and steep.

Good relationships are built upon stable foundations, so be a rock unto yourself and become a rock for others.

Accept sovereignty over your life and achieve the highest authority on Earth, knowing that to rule truly is to serve. At times we all need a touchstone – a stable influence in our lives that we can rely upon, someone who will not judge us, nor try to change us.

To be a rock one must bring stillness, constancy and stability to an otherwise changing landscape. So when others behave badly, don't lower yourself through behaving badly also, and don't let pride undermine the foundations of who you are.

Your companions need you to have the strength to allow them to make mistakes. When relationships fall upon troubled times, someone must hold the centre, their strength and devotion will empower the others. Without this, relationships split apart.

When you are inwardly centered and strong, and outwardly kind and gentle, others will see their reflection in you and with respect for your humility they will return your devotion in good time.

Purple/Turquoise   Mountain/Lake
Initiation

Mountain reflected in the Lake: this is a time for reflection, to question appearances, and commit to one's true path.

These Runes call you to refine your character, question your attachments, and make sacrifices, letting go of the things that hold you back.

Are you attached to:

Relationships that damage your self-esteem?

The need for other people's approval?

Plans, ideas, ideals?

Sidetracks rather than your own true path?

Fear about not having enough, or the desire to have more?

This is a time of initiation. These hard times are just a phase; a test for you to find the strength of character to be who you truly are, to love who your truly are, and to do what must be done.

Simplify your life now and search for your inner truth. If appearances need to suffer for simplicity's sake, then so be it. Don't make choices for the sake of appearances. Have faith and take a risk, don't be guided by fear.

Other people will not understand what is going on, they may demand things of you that are inappropriate, so be true to yourself and safeguard your dignity.

Your Ego will also question your judgement, calling you delusional, for your actions may appear to be impractical, irrational, naive, and selfish.

Be strong in the face of adversity, for when you make the sacrifice, providence will move you towards a time and place of abundance.

Purple/White   Mountain/Heaven
Service through Wisdom

Heaven in the Mountain is like a room filled with gold, an alchemical chamber where life's experiences are filtered and processed in a personal cauldron of wisdom.

These Runes call you to cultivate the wisdom to be of service in other people's lives. Through Mountain you come to know yourself and you choose what to believe. Mountain brings a contemplative quality to the controlling mechanisms of Heaven, to quiet the Will so choices can be made that reflect the truer aspects of oneself. Then one's reality is built upon firm foundations.

This is the school room of your creative potential. Here you gain insights, collect your thoughts, filter and process them, for greater understanding to precede your actions. Here you cultivate the wisdom to serve a community of interest in which you have a common bond, you learn to know who to associate with and when it is appropriate to offer help, holding knowledge to your centre until others are receptive and open to your influence.

Before contributing to the lives of others you must assimilate what you will pass on, accepting your life's experiences as building blocks for your education as a helpful person.

You must know yourself in relation to what you experience, for everything that matters in your life is mirrored by the people, things and places that enter your circle of experience.

Cultivating the wisdom to help others requires dedication to the development of one's own character. Through understanding your compassion will grow. So take responsibility for your central position in all that happens and be conscious of the way your life is shaped by your relationships with all things.

Be strong enough to hold your centre.

Purple/Blue   Mountain/Water
Guiding Wisdom

These Runes call you to seek the highest good, to pay attention to the Wisdom along your way, imparting Wisdom when it is called for and listening when it is given.

Life's journey is an apprenticeship requiring enthusiasm, dedication and receptivity to guidance. Many times in life you are delivered into situations you must learn from. Consider your approach: when lacking experience, seek out a teacher; something or someone to inspire and help you shape and follow your vision.

The way to learn is through experience: learn from your mistakes so the same lessons need not be repeated over again.

One's character develops with thoroughness and dedication to this path. The foolish quit just before the end, or they go too far, not heeding the lessons and the warnings along the way.

The journey starts by asking the right questions of oneself. If one seeks to manipulate the truth or is unintelligent in questioning, then misguidance or misfortune may result.

Those who walk with innocence seek the right advice.

We all have authority and others can learn from our experience, so the teacher we seek and the teacher we are should know how to impart wisdom.

The Mountain, like the wise hermit of fairytale and myth, gathers its wisdom through contemplation and waits for the seekers and the lost to call.

People only listen to good advice when they are ready. When we are ready to teach we should be ready to take our own advice, for often we counsel what we need most ourselves.

Both teacher and student benefit by seeing in each other their mutual reflections.

The wise may wear the mask of a fool, so don't let appearances deceive you. See through the masks people wear and take a deeper look at the things and places along your way.

Everything you need to find lies on your path, so pay attention to the signs that guide you, and to the things people say, for the Divine works through paradox.

What you need to see most clearly will often come in disguise.

Green/Clear   **Thunder/Unity**
Your Creation Story

Life is a never-ending story, its themes are passed from one life to the next and from one generation to another. Our beliefs are built upon the stories we inherit from our ancestors, our parents, and our past lives. They set the scene for our lives through religion, social conventions, myths and scientific facts. We hear it, we see it, we rethink it, and then we say it is so – and so it is.

Through our stories we guide our world into existence, playing our part in the Divine act of creation.

Longing motivates our lives, we experience separation and we long to close the gap, to experience belonging, and to feel that we are whole.

We journey along a holy road. Holiness means wholeness. The journey towards wholeness requires no convention. We are all built uniquely for the journey.

With longing in our hearts we follow our calling to the end of the road. The road can be as long and hard as you want to make it. The road somehow seems shorter when our life's story is filled with wonder and joy.

A good story takes us closer to the realisation of who we are, where we are, and how we are being.

Use *The Glass Runes Oracle* to help you follow your story line, to wander and wonder through the inner landscape of your life and home.

What is written in your script? Are you sick and tired of the same old story? Your biography soon becomes your biology, and it can make you sick. Perhaps it is time to change a line, substitute a word, or start over again?

Have faith in yourself, be authentic, speak your truth and follow your heartfelt calling. In Genesis the story goes: *"and God said let there be light... and there was light"*. God is in the words of your story and in the details of your home. Speak your truth and walk your talk, for your words have the power to transform your life.

When you entered this world they told you its stories. You live within the context of their stories and you create your life around what you believe. When you depart this world, what will you be remembered for? What story would you have them tell?

You are the author.

Green/Green   *Thunder/Thunder*
The Wake-up Call

We journey with fate to overcome many obstacles.

Life requires movement, flow and change, so we must be flexible in body and mind to greet our opportunities no matter what form they come in and no matter how shocking they appear to be.

At a difficult crossroads, Soul calls your heart to go the right way, but doubt says give in to what you fear and go another way.

To discover an untruth about your life is shocking enough, but often fate delivers a blow to turn our lives upside down and disorientate our points of view.

Shocks can be an awakening. They may awaken you from a dream and cast you into a living nightmare, or into circumstances that seem beyond your control.

Things are no longer the way they were the night before. Something behind the scenes has plotted a different course for you.

Whatever troubles you is your friend, it wants to help you out, to move beyond whatever is holding you back. Troubles occupy your life as a lodger, they will not go away until you recognise the message they bring, and if you don't they will follow you around, returning time after time and each time more shocking than the last.

Welcome your adversity and try to see the bigger picture. To do this you must keep the shock external. Don't get caught up in the turmoil of change it brings, hold a strong and steady center to be fully present and awake to what is going on.

Victims of circumstance harbour resentment and anger and their lives become hardened – don't let this happen to you. Don't be a loser, for this drains your life of energy and you become weak.

Be a warrior through whatever circumstance you find yourself. Your Spirit is victorious, it knows how to battle and where to go, but you must choose what path to take, you are the spiritual director of your own life story.

When people harden, something about them dies, so yield to what life brings, bless it all, be flexible and forgiving, for Love is life's disciple.

Green/Orange   *Thunder/Wind*
Living with your Story

Thunder and Wind are the forces that move you, they give you the power and motivation to choose your creative direction and lead the way that determines your fate.

These Runes call you to know that you are the author and creative director of your whole life story, but there are things you cannot change. You cannot change the bedrock upon which you build your life, you cannot change the positions of the planets nor the elemental qualities imbedded in the foundations of who you are.

By Divine design some things seek you out and some things must take form in your life. In the act of creation you simply work with the elements life gives you, playing the cards that you are dealt.

Thunder and Wind direct your life on a path of achievement.

You search for more Love, more knowledge, more comfort, more power, and when having more fails to satisfy, you redefine what you are after and realign your path.

The Divine paradox is a sign at the end of the road that says, "less is more". When we get there having walked the sidetracks of delusion, discontent, frustration and impatience, we know by that time that we have gone about things in the wrong way or for the wrong reasons. If what you do is dictated by your mood swings and not by the enduring actions of your character, then what you experience in life will push and pull you from your steady path.

To achieve simplicity in life we must first deal with life's complexities, for we find ourselves caught in its tangled web. Cutting ties and letting go of things that are not on your path will help you free yourself from bondage, but your strongest attachment is to your story. Detach yourself to see the bigger picture, for you play the leading role in the script of your design. Tune into the subscript, its undercurrent runs through the bedrock of your life and guides you to be authentic, honest and fair when dealing with the people, places and things you meet along the way.

Green/Red   Thunder/Fire
Authenticity

Fire is your truth and sincerity, and it is also the image you present to the world. Thunder is your authority and the influence you have in the world. Thunder and Fire put you in the spotlight so that you can be seen and heard.

These Runes call you to consider times when you become the focus of attention. You must be sensitive in managing this position of influence.

People are open to hearing what you say as long as you are sincere and do not judge them.

People are sensitive to authority, they will remain open to you as long as they can warm to your sincerity and you do not take advantage of their attention. Respect is lost through forcing opinions, telling lies and being manipulative.

When you are open to others and true to yourself your light shines through, then it comes naturally to say and do the right things.

To be authentic means to speak as your true self without playing roles or wearing masks. When you are being authentic others, are not judged by you, you do not place them in a role that suits your story, and you see through any role they might be playing. You see their light, and have compassion for who they are.

Many conditions hold us back from being who we truly are.

The journey of belonging is a journey to discover one's authentic self and to feel content with one's place in the world. This is a journey that takes a whole lifetime, but along the way, windows of opportunity open for us to illuminate our lives with the truth of our own experience and to help other people find their way when they are open to our influence.

Green/Yellow   *Thunder/Earth*
Everyday hero

Blink your eye and capture this moment.

These Runes call you to be less in your story and more in your life – to be the true hero of the moment. Once the story kicks in you have a past, present and future. Without the story everything is perfect right here, right now.

It is difficult to be in the moment all the time, most of the time we inhabit our stories. Your stories are your ego's playground. It wants a good part to play in a commanding performance, it wants to know what scene is coming next, to know its place, and its lines, it looks forward to a good ending, and to taking some credit.

Spending so much time in your wanna-be someone and wanna-be somewhere role, trapped within your story, you don't realise you are already the hero. Ego watches every move, a nit-picking editor stealing the beauty from each moment, diverting your attention elsewhere.

Pause, breathe in, and blink your eyes. How wonderful is this moment and how wonderful are you in this moment? Now how long was it before the editor was in your face again putting you down, that voice inside saying that you have lost the plot and who do you think you are. The ego's editor is insecure, it wants to keep you in your place. But we are out there looking at you, we want to know who you truly are, we want the natural one, the shining one, the one who is brave enough to take a chance and gracious when receiving our applause. We don't want to see a pale imitation – our hearts are searching for the true hero, because we also want to be more courageous and enthusiastic in our everyday lives.

The true hero makes the final and greatest sacrifice when he/she has no more resistance to life. There is no escaping this, be it through wisdom or through illness, we will eventually surrender, for our Soul is seeking experience not applause.

Green/Turquoise   Thunder/Lake
Influential Behaviour

Lake yields to the influence of Thunder like a gently bubbling cauldron mixing the ingredients of life's story. Beneath the surface its qualities endure, above the surface shimmering waves form to follow joyously in Thunder's wake.

These Runes call you to pay attention to the choices you make in relation to your own authority and the authority of others, to pay attention to the honest management of your own power, and to do it joyously, without injury to self-esteem.

They prompt you to follow the calling of your heart and be mindful that in offering some aspect of your innocence to a relationship that will change your life you do not give up what is essentially yours.

When you commit to follow or to honour others, make sure you continue to honour yourself.

If you find yourself in a position of influence consider what drives your attitude here. Are you being honest, respecting the boundaries of the other person, place or thing? When self-sacrifice is driven by the ego there is a loss of spirit because the ego holds on to the need to control the situation, expecting something in return.

If others influence you or you influence them, consider if there are hidden agendas, and what is really at stake here? For the answer you must reach beneath the surface of appearances and desires. If you prostitute your values it will hurt your self-esteem. Are your actions the way truly to love yourself?

Green/White   Thunder/Heaven
Management of Power

These Runes call you to know the power of your own authority and to direct your power to where it will most benefit your life's calling.

Through the correct management of power, conditions are in unity with Heaven's order. Mismanagement and the abuse of power further the great pretence, and in these troubled times the false faces of wisdom, virtue and morality maintain an unhealthy status quo.

We live in troubled times. There is so much we all could do, but only certain things that we are each meant to. You must decide where to direct your attention, for where thoughts go energy follows. In this way you direct your power.

Each one of us is powerful, we can all achieve what is meant to be in this life, but our choices determine whether we will. When the things we consider and the things we do are not in our best interests we are depleted, having less energy to channel into the things that really matter in our lives.

Consider how to use your influence justly and to establish the right order in your life through what you think, say and do.

Find the right way through perseverance, not strife or force, for the use of force is disempowering because it ties one into the process of conflict and its resolution.

The balance of power is forever shifting and should never be taken for granted, because over-confidence fosters misjudgement, channelling energy into thoughts and commitments that do not serve one's higher purpose.

Consider your self-worth and commit only to act honourably. This is the empowering way to conserve your energy for appropriate causes.

Green/Blue   Thunder/Water
Moving on

Thunder rolls across the landscape of our lives, sweeping clean the past and clearing the air, then rain falls like tears of forgiveness and we are free to move on.

These Runes call you to bless the influences of your past, for they help to shape the way you are. Forgive the transgressions of others and cut the ties that stop you moving on.

Now it is time to change the habits and the friends that feed your unhealthy addictions. A clean sweep should be made as quickly as possible, followed by time out to recuperate and review.

Some people, places and things are constant in our lives, while others will come and go.

The seeds of the new are carried in the old, so learn what you can from the past and give up the attachments that do not serve you and the addictions that hold you back, for unnecessary baggage is a burden.

Do not dwell on failings, simply let them pass, and forgive the misdeeds of others, for everything in your life is part of who you are; essential ingredients that mould and shape your existence. With an open heart, move on.

> Last night I dreamed
> - Blessed illusion -
> That I had a beehive here in my heart
> and that
> The golden bees were making white combs
> and sweet honey from my old failures.
>
> John O' Donohue

Green/Purple   Thunder/Mountain
Small is Beautiful

Thunder on the Mountain conditions your point of view.

These Runes call you to experience a wonderful life in the people, places and things you sometimes take for granted.

When Thunder claps on the Mountain, prudence is necessary, for it is unwise to set out upon big tasks; better to progress with smaller things closer to home.

Quiet your mind and your voice, and take a closer look at life.

The wise know that "God is in the details". They say: "Small is beautiful," and they see the world in a grain of sand. Some people do not have this perspective. Lacking a sense of awe they cannot see this point of view.

A storm will brew when you enter another's house to give them advice they did not call for. One cannot be forced to see things in a different way, so it is better at this time to stay at home and take your own advice.

In meekness you will find beauty, comfort, and strength, so don't overlook the people and things that seem to be insignificant, modest, or withdrawn from view.

Beware of those who blow their trumpets loudly, and rescue yourself when climbing too high, and dominating others' points of view. Just pay attention to the small things, and be conscientious in doing what must be done.

Orange/Clear   *Wind/Unity*
Yield and Overcome

Stillness at the center of the twister.

Keep your center whilst the winds of change blow all about you.

Meet the challenges of this time as the willow meets the howling wind: gently flexing and yielding to the challenges on your way.

Progress without striving, gaining without force.

Driving from the centre around which all things spin.

Orange/Orange   *Wind/Wind*
Creative Direction

Two Winds blow, filling the sails and setting the direction.

You are the author and the creative director of your own life story.

The author writes the script and the creative director manages the process.

These Runes call you to be efficient, consistent and gentle in managing the course of your life.

Go only where you need to, do only what needs to be done, and trust in the Divine for guidance. Set your course to go where the true Wind blows you, it knows your destination and the surest direction.

If you try to sail the opposite way you will fail, if you tack from side to side, deviating from the steady path, your journey will be hard to sustain, and you will arrive late and exhausted.

You are the navigator and pioneer, going where no one has gone before. You know there is a purpose to your journey and a destination you must reach, you have a vision of where you are going. To follow that vision is your goal.

To start you must have a plan, not a firm plan cast in stone, but a fluid plan that you can monitor and change along the way. You need the self-discipline to track your own progress whilst keeping an eye on your ego as it tries to undermine your commitment to your higher purpose and your chosen path.

The forces of habit, stubborn pride, driving ambition and burning desire will test your resolve to be true to yourself and your calling.

Watch yourself as you try to force the pace and sabotage your vision and your plan, but make your actions gentle yet decisive, for when there is commitment, providence moves the winds to fill the sails.

Orange/Red   Wind/Fire
Harmony in the Family

The spirit of life flows through the family tree.

These Runes call you to bring harmony to your family.

Our essence or spirit flows within our past, present, and future, beyond the boundaries of time and place, connecting threads to weave the web of life.

We live amongst the patterns that connect our present life with our past and future ones, and with the lives of our ancestors and offspring.

The essence of a family is reborn into each new life, returned from the primal womb into another chapter of family life, until its end and the return to innocence once more, rejoining brothers and sisters in the space beyond creation.

Social harmony within the world is born from harmony within the family.

Start at home and foster within yourself and your family the influences you want to see grow into society.

Develop your personal nature by weeding out unhealthy habits and traits conditioned by your past. Through healing yourself you send healing through your family tree.

Each member plays a vital part in the healthy life of their family, each must find the self-discipline to honour their place, and to help others take their place in the web of life.

Influence should come from within and work outwards, for

what you say will have lasting effect when backed up by your own conduct.

Orange/Yellow   Wind/Earth
Creative Thinking

Wind gently penetrates to the heart of what matters in your life so you may see your world the way it is. Change your view then your experience will change too.

These Runes call you to care for what you think. Negative emotions damage your body and break you down, positive affirmations take you closer to what you want.

Life is your present. It is made up of moments, so welcome whatever happens in each moment as if you had chosen it yourself. Even the most challenging moments are a gift, so accept them graciously, looking beneath the surface wrapping and the words to find the treasure inside.

Get to know your own mind, for you are its creative director.

Watch yourself as you cast your thoughts into other people's business, back to the past and into the future, as you direct your mind to become the judge, the jury and the executioner. Watch your thoughts as they become emotional and harden into your body causing physical pain.

Your thinking is a companion that should be given only a little space in your life, for when the mind is full of thoughts it cannot see the signs nor hear the inspirations that try to guide your way. Silence your mind to make room for peace, love, and joy to enter.

Your thoughts are seeds cast into the landscape of your life. Weed out the destructive ones and cultivate the creative ones.

Understand the heart of what matters and let truth rain down upon you to cleanse your motivation and bring clarity to your judgement.

Transcend the limitations of argument to find truth in how you really feel.

Celebrate your differences, and see to it that your uniqueness takes its place in the world. We are all complementary parts of a greater whole. "Vive la différence!"

Orange/Turquoise   *Wind/Lake*
Inner Truth

The Wind stirs reflections in the Lake, gently penetrating the surface of appearances. The world at the surface is a shallow place, a veneer of the way things really are.

Here it appears there are those who have, and those who have not; wealth, it seems, is abundance, and beauty is only skin deep. Position in society, possessions, and how one appears to others have all become emblems of worthiness, crowning glories worn to signify stature in the world of illusions.

These Runes call you to look beyond the world of facades and to see beyond the masks that people wear.

When making judgements they ask you to be free from prejudice, and to open your heart to the truth beyond appearances, to be yourself and allow others to be who they are, forgiving their transgressions and accepting your own imperfections.

Situations and people change, but we have no right to expect each other to change, all we can do is to work upon our own position with honour and compassion.

When it is time to take action it must be done fairly with true understanding, penetrating the depths of every situation with an open mind in search of the truth, looking for something positive to build upon.

Orange/White   *Wind/Heaven*
Empowering Reserve

Heaven's Wind draws clouds across the sky, transient images engaging the imagination. Their temporary form can neither be grasped nor measured.

Similarly, at this time you must see your current situation as transient, a time to pause and wonder at what is going on in your life.

These Runes call you to look inward, to question what is real and refine your way of seeing and your way of being.

The situation you are in at the moment cannot be controlled by your will. Trying to take control or to have things your way simply aggravates the situation. In forcing an issue you are breaking your own honour code. Try to step back from the situation to see the bigger picture.

What is the most honourable way that you can act?
What will it take for you to surrender to the situation?

Don't dwell on what you do and what you achieve. Follow the calling of your Soul, and return to the cradle of your innocence to refine the expression of your nature in small ways.

Heaven's Wind penetrates the places of your life where longing lives, moving you to feel your Soul calling and to choose a better way to live through your experience.

It calls for you to be gentle, adaptable and ready to do what must be done with honour and dignity. This is the only way to achieve the right outcome.

Orange/Blue   *Wind/Water*
The Way of Energy

Wind over Water – Moving energy in the journey of your life.

These Runes call you to understand the way that spiritual energy manifests in the landscape of your life, to live in harmony with the creative force that shapes your experience, and to have more faith and greater acceptance, surrendering to its flow.

Life's creative energy cannot be seen nor touched, it flows throughout the invisible landscapes of our bodies, minds and homes, through hidden streams (meridians) that animate the physical matter of body and land, through the imagination of the collective unconscious that animates our thoughts and dreams, and through what we perceive to be time and space.

This energy we call *Ki, Chi, Prana, and Spirit,* moves and shapes the physical world, affecting all our thoughts and emotions, working beneath the surface of all appearances.

A great healer shifts this energy to improve its flow, a great warrior moves with it and projects it, creative thinkers tap into it for inspiration and wisdom.

When *Ki* does not flow freely, life does not go smoothly and it is hard to achieve what must be done; therefore root out the places where *Ki* is blocked in your body, your home, and your whole life story.

Fulfill your life where it feels empty and clear your life where it feels stuck; learn to go with its flow.

Compassion and understanding heal resentment and alienation by dissolving differences that block the flow. It is better to resolve a problem before it hardens or grows out of proportion.

Pride comes before the fall. Prevention is better than cure.

Orange/Purple   *Wind/Mountain*
Centering

We move through life riding the wheel of change. At the centre of the wheel there is stillness, and all things spin around the centre. Often we get caught up in the movement, losing our centre and being carried along by circumstances.

Wind calls you to be an individual, to express yourself and cut your path in the world. Mountain calls you to the higher aspect of who you are; it aids your personal development and your code of honour.

You must work on making the right moves. The only way to move is from the center. All other movement requires too much force.

Force an issue and it will not be well received, force the pace and others will tire of you. You do not have the energy to progress by force.

Being centered is a quality of Mountain. In this state you benefit from the high ground, seeing the bigger picture and enjoying the sanctuary of stillness.

When you position yourself correctly your feet are firmly planted and you are able to adapt to whatever comes your way.

With commitment to this way of being, providence will guide your movements.

When you lose your footing you get caught up in the movement like a wanderer who cannot find his way home.

Conserve your energy and direct it where it counts – you cannot fight every battle and win every race. Some things are meant for you and others are not.

Develop your perception to rise above what is going on in your life. Wait patiently and make yourself ready and receptive to what is coming your way.

When ego controls your movements you lose your centre. Ego in its adolescence just wants to be out there. Ego fears that time is against you.

Your higher self knows that time and fate are on your side. Don't listen to your ego, attune yourself to the silence and stillness at the center, then you will make the right moves in life.

Movement from this state of well-being is gentle and penetrating, and the changes that follow are enduring.

Orange/Green   *Wind/Thunder*
Achieving what is Meant to Be

Thunder adds its power to Wind, prospering your endeavours when the motives you set are right.

These Runes call you to accomplish something great now that fate will lend a hand. Success is assured as a natural consequence at this time of selfless deeds.

With the right attitude even unfortunate events will lead to prosperity. Make the most of this time while it lasts.

You are not the driving force, but the mediator. Furthering your cause is a blessing that suits a higher plan. You must pass the blessing on, knowing that this abundance is prospered through sharing.

Surrender yourself humbly to your position, need nothing in

return for kindness, and act honourably towards others, accepting their limitations, forgiving their mistakes and not setting yourself above another, for no position is immune to misfortune's return.

Loosen your grip on the steering-wheel, the hand of fate takes the controls along the road to self-betterment.

Red/Clear   *Fire/Unity*
Let there be Light

When life becomes heavy and hard and darkness descends, awaken your spark, ignite your Fire to soften the contrasts and lighten your load.

The heavy, hard and dark are garments you wear and curtains you draw across the landscape of your life.

Your body is light, your being is light, and when you look for direction you are looking for the light.

We all shine, but not everyone around us can recognise this, so be happy to illuminate the lives of those who can see you, and for those that cannot – just simply shine.

When you cover yourself with false image, deceit and pretence, you shroud your life-force and something about you begins to die.

Your light is true, direct, warm, passionate, soft and loving. In your true light you are truly sexy, you are compassionate, radiant and divine.

First see yourself in your true light then others will see you that way.

At times you will reach the shore when others are still out at sea. Be the light on the shore so they may find their way.

When you are natural you can breathe easily and you have less to think about. Being natural requires less energy than being false.

Take the high road to what you are seeking. Perhaps there is realisation, love or enlightenment on your horizon.

You need to be light to rise above your problems, heal your ailments and transcend the things that hold you down.

"Let there be light" is a call to be truly alive, and a call for celebration. Look on the bright side of life, you are a star, so shine.

Take yourself lightly and make light of your situation.

Love the way you look, love the way you feel and sound, love the way you smell, the stories you have to tell and the things you love to taste.

Life is love – love your life.

Red/Red   *Fire/Fire*
The Tears of a Clown

Two lights on the horizon – so you may find your way through pleasure and pain.

These Runes call you to know your heart and to think with your heart, for this is how you will find what you are looking for.

Heaven calls and Earth provides the things that matter in our lives. Fire lights the way so we may find truth and love whilst following our calling and doing what must be done.

Life can be a merry dance, for we dance to the rhythm of our own drum. In the school of life we must welcome both pleasure and pain as an education of the heart, for we will experience pain many times on the road to achieving something great.

The wise man and the fool walk the true path together. When the wise man sees the light he questions his heart, when the fool sees the light he laughs out loud and sees the lighter side to his tragedy and the joy waiting at the other side of pain. The fool is not a clown for he has nothing to hide, no concern about what other people think and no desire to capture attention, he simply is the way he is and goes his merry way.

At the end of the journey the wise man is happy to be a fool and the fool knows he is wise, whilst clowns dance in the company of clowns masking the way they feel inside.

The masks we wear hide our authenticity and are never a good fit.

Red/Yellow   *Fire/Earth*
Forward in Abundance

The Divine light of Fire shines brightly above the smog of Earthly illusion, seeking an invitation to break through, to guide the way with inspiration and abundance. Earthly pleasures and knowledge are comforting, but real progress is made when the Divine light guides the way.

These Runes call you to know the way towards rapid easy

progress, with ever widening expansion and clarity.

Your progress is good and the way forward is promising. The material world can provide all that is needed for your earthly comfort and sensual pleasure, but there is more.

The ultimate path towards abundance requires that you become unattached to opinions and possessions, to see more clearly through Divine inspiration.

Cleverness is not the way to enlightenment, and amassing things to call your own will not provide enduring wealth.

To be blessed with abundance you must be abundant in how you walk your talk, leading by your own example. Get out of your own way by just doing what needs to be done without being attached to the outcome. Let go of the need to know, and of the need to force your opinion.

Abundance is gifted to you, governed by a higher authority, so you must recognise you do not walk alone.

An abundant attitude is a generous one, it maintains a healthy balance between the wisdom and wealth one holds and the wisdom and wealth one shares.

Red/Turquoise   Fire/Lake
Meeting Opposition

The external influence of Fire as the light that guides your way is far off and therefore dim.

Others stand in the light, not recognising you and misunderstanding you. Shadows are cast across the surface of the Lake, but beneath the surface a light shines brightly.

The path is lit for you to find your way in the depths of who you are.

These Runes call you to find your own way in the light of opposition, to say what you really believe even though you may be misunderstood or not heard.

Other people will test your self-esteem, your resolve to be true to yourself. The challenge is to seek your own counsel on how to preserve your individuality, confronting the oppositions you find within yourself, and taking a soft approach with those who appear to stand in your way.

Don't be led astray by the influence of others. You give away your power by wearing the mask that it suits someone else to look at, and by behaving in a way to satisfy others.

It is empowering to find your own way to rise above the situation. The push for recognition at this stage requires the use of too much force, which will not serve you in the long run. You must seek success in small matters that will build towards a result that endures.

No force is needed to resolve your internal conflicts and misunderstandings. You must take the path of least resistance and find the strength to persevere in this task, learning from all the mistakes and misunderstandings along your way.

As the truth of your situation unfolds, your path will become lighter and you will find more encouragement.

Red/White   *Fire/Heaven*
Sharing your Light

Fire in Heaven sends light into the world.

These Runes call you to know: you are a gift to the world and the world is a gift to you. Your light is your inheritance, shining through you, to be developed and made present in the world.

The world needs your presence, because you can make a difference. Even if your abilities are limited, and your talents are small, you are blessed with special qualities that shine through the things you do.

You cannot know the final effect of the words you say and the actions you take, these are ripples that make a significant difference to the lives of others. So encourage truth and love to shine in your life, in this way you will find your Calling, and Heaven's bidding will be done.

Life is a journey of discovery – as you walk towards your truth your light becomes clear, and as your light becomes clear the lives of others are illuminated by yours.

Fire shines its light on all, no matter how they behave. It makes both good and evil visible in the world.

Recognise that all people are gifted, each with a unique way of delivering light into the world. Accept people for who they are, for despite our actions we all walk in the same light. With understanding and forgiveness we illuminate each other's lives.

Red/Blue   *Fire/Water*
Prepare for Change

With Fire above and Water below, the conditions for growth are set. Fire brings clarity and Water brings direction. These Runes call you to pay attention to the time preceding new beginnings when outmoded aspects of your life have had their day.

At the start of a new project or a new aspect of life, it seems there is a lot to do – things are not how you would like them to be, but within the apparent disorder of what is to come order is already implicit.

Each new matter you will deal with brings another aspect of growth to your life. This is the hidden gift within the things that are to come.

You need to be cautious and well prepared. You cannot carry unfinished business and unfinished projects into this new territory.

At the beginning of a journey you must be light enough for travel, because you will gather new things along the way. Here you are called to cut the ties with outmoded ways of being.

Clarity must precede effort. Before proceeding into this new territory it is wise to get a good vantage point from which you can see the bigger picture.

Clarity is only possible through a peaceful state of mind. Through this state you can find the light of inner truth with which to guide your way, and once the journey begins you must keep this light in sight.

It is tempting to find comfort in the shadows and to linger in this place for too long. Then the new territory is yet another step away.

The more solace you find in your shadows the more baggage you carry. The heavier you become the harder it is to climb to the place where you can have a better outlook on your life.

Red/Purple   Fire/Mountain
Longing

On the journey through life we long to find our way back to the Mountain. Mountain is our inner home. Fire is the light that guides the way through the inner and outer landscapes of our lives.

These Runes call you to know that longing is a heartfelt Calling of the Soul to find your way back home.

Sometimes you lose your way, don't follow your light, and become sidetracked, then the Divine presents meaningful encounters in an attempt to put you back on track.

Straying far from your true path you meet adversity, then Fire illuminates your experience with the insight to stop and realign your life.

Feeling settled is a feeling of inner harmony when the heart and mind are at peace. When you feel you don't fit in or you lack direction, feel ungrounded and discontent, then you have lost your connection with your inner home.

It is better to follow your inner light than to look for satisfaction in external things, for other people and places will never fulfil your deeper sense of longing.

Everything is felt in our inner world, every step we take in the outer world affects our inner home. Even when an adversary enters your outer circle you can find a place for him in your heart, but when you judge yourself and others you build a prison deep inside.

Learn to have a lighter touch – the ability to touch people's lives and then move on, to be centred in your approach, gentle, modest, adaptable and cheerful, knowing how to meet changing situations, secure in your belonging, at home within yourself.

A fire on the mountain is a temporary pleasure: like a travelling minstrel it brings light relief and then it is gone. Those who are arrogant, aloof or guarded cannot touch the hearts of others, and their journey is lonely because others do not welcome them in.

Red/Green   Fire/Thunder
Justice as a Teacher

Thunder and lightning wake us up with a clap to sharpen our senses and a flash of realisation.

These Runes call you to be just and true in managing your authority with clarity, love and forgiveness.

We author our lives through the choices we make, knowing there are consequences for every action.

The way of love and truth brings light, so walk in the light and have nothing to fear. When we stray from our true path, lacking respect for others or becoming self-serving in our pursuits, we darken our light and the spirit calls for realisation to enter our lives, to refocus our attention on what is right, to realise the error of our ways. Sometimes the experience of loss or pain is a chance to reflect, realign ourselves and then move on.

If you are drawn into the spotlight of authority, it is time to question your allegiance to the truth. Take a vow to be true to yourself and to follow your true calling.

At times we are called to stand up for the truth and to help another see the error of their ways. Be sure that you have this authority, for to be fair one has to keep some distance from the issue, and put aside one's personal feelings.

It is not fair to be angry, to seek vengeance or a tit-for-tat exchange of pain and power. Justice comes from seeing the situation objectively in its true light, with consideration for the other points of view.

Clear and decisive action is called for. Bring the matter to a conclusion and let there be forgiveness, so that the end may be followed by a new beginning. A penalty should be a deterrent and a wake-up call, not a punishment.

Through making mistakes and taking the wrong direction we

experience the consequences of our actions and learn to correct ourselves.

In one way or another we are all accountable for our actions, so have a moderate attitude towards transgressions, for good leadership is born from respect, not fear.

Red/Orange *Fire/Wind*
Sacred Vessels

Wind fills the bellows and drives the Fire to illuminate the story of your life. It animates the sacred vessels of your personal identity, body and home, and drives you forward on a journey to discover meaning, belonging and wholeness.

Fire is your truth, Calling to you like a beacon at the horizon of your life. It sparks your quest to journey through the Invisible Landscape: to enter your shadows and engage your demons, to triumph over adversity and do what must be done.

These Runes call you to become the hero of your own life story, to explore your life and find what you are looking for.

The Divine guides you through the details of your life: your physical health, your attitudes and beliefs, and the place in which you live all hold messages to help you on your journey.

Your Calling is your sacred quest to act with honour and dignity and to follow your true path towards your destiny. In this way you become the hero of your own life story, and what you achieve for yourself benefits society as a whole.

Every person, place and thing that enters your circle of belonging brings a new experience to your life, a new opportunity to move closer toward home. When the experience is difficult or painful you are called to go deeper, to enter the wound and find the source of the pain: first to see it and then to heal it through forgiveness.

In this way you purify your life, and through purification you find the enlightened way home.

Yellow/Clear   *Earth/Unity*
Following the Light

Is life just a journey or is it a pilgrimage? We find ourselves here looking for something. "Something is missing or not quite right, something is out of place – or is it me?" You ask yourself: "Am I doing something wrong, why do these things happen to me, why do I behave this way, why am I discontent?"

On a pilgrimage, one is devoted to the path. The pilgrim walks with faith in the path, and so we must walk with faith in our paths.

Each of us has a horizon, and upon it there is hope like a beacon illuminating the way. So that is where we set our sights, hope guides us to the people, places and things that might bring happiness, we meet them along the way, and with each step we move towards the truth about our lives.

Our meetings and our relationships by necessity are challenging, for each obstacle or problem in life is an opportunity for growth. Personal growth creates the ripples that make the waves of change in the great ocean of life through which we are all connected.

We want our lives to be lighter, more fun, happier and healthier, but often it is hard to find it here, down to earth, grounded, sometimes feeling like a prisoner of this place and time. So we try to escape, we go up in our heads chasing dreams or answers, away with the fairies or out of our minds, or we hide in the shadows or behind the masks and the facades that life gives us, afraid of judgement, though judging others from a distance.

Life is an enchanted journey, each step a meditation. With each step you place yourself in the world, down to earth, at home in the moment. Always look up from where you are because there is always light on your horizon: glimmers of hope reach out to you, love and truth try to break through.

The true nature of every person, place and thing is radiant, innocent and beautiful; but often we only see the masks, the shadows and the facades. The light inside is not so obvious, but it is always there. There are no bad people, only misguided ones, those who do not follow their light.

Walk in your light, walk in peace, taking care, having respect, and walking lightly, blessing everyone in their goodness, and blessing yourself: for blessing is the road towards freedom.

Yellow/Yellow   *Earth/Earth*
What is the Matter

The sacred vessels of body, home and nature give us residence and cradle our lives. They tell our story for they are microcosms of all that happens, reflections of all that matters in our life.

These Runes call you to recognise that spirit animates your choices to make your feelings and thoughts part of your physical experience; it gives them form in the fabric of your material world. You arrive at every place through the choices you make and surround yourself with things that embody some aspect of your life story.

Soul calls to you to take a look at yourself intimately through the mirror of your experience, considering the people, places and things you associate with as mirrors of the way you are. Look at them and tell yourself: "Into me I see".

The body and the home are open and receptive to become animated by spirit. So if the spirit suffers the body and home will suffer also. The problems in the home and ailments of the body are opportunities to tune into the creative calling of your life.

We carry our thoughts and our things with us through our lives, some of them make life easier, more comfortable and happy – all of them are companions. They have something to offer; if not comfort, happiness and ease then perhaps awakening to what is inappropriate.

Through your thoughts and actions you invest yourself in our future, so make yours a fertile place sowing seeds to be helpful and productive. Don't let stagnation set into your life, for much that ails the body and causes problems in the home stems from unresolved issues lurking in the shadows of the psyche.

Yellow/Turquoise   **Earth/Lake**
Nature and Nurture

Through the Lake we may perceive the depths of our belonging.

These Runes call you to know yourself as the guardian of your innocence, mother of your genius and teacher in your circle of belonging.

Look beyond the mirror to see your innocence and to find the guardian wisdom of the mother teacher. Let sensitivity, in-tuition and love guide you to bring your genius into the world, and to see genius in others.

To hold a child too tightly or too long for fear that they might make the wrong move, or walk in harm's way, is smothering. We must give others and ourselves the space to develop relationships with life through love of who we are, where we are, and what we perceive.

We are all children in this wonderland we call earth. Hold your circle of belonging in an open and comforting embrace, so all that enter may draw from the wellspring of your knowledge and experience.

Help us children to see more deeply into the depths of who we are, so we may learn to greet the thresholds of our lives without fear of change, but stand at their edge with open hearts and minds. This embrace is intimate, for when I am held in this way, into-me-I-see.

The well from which your wisdom springs is an eye filled with tears. All the tears of joy and pain waiting to greet us at the thresholds of our lives fill this place, it is the cradle of belonging in the womb of the Soul.

Soul animates our lives with windows of opportunity to see our wounds as places to visit, not places to dwell, for beyond the wound there is always a new horizon.

Develop inner sight so the warmth of your wisdom will bring your genius to the surface. Open your arms, your eyes and your heart to what you perceive, for short-sighted ignorance confines one's longing to the shadows of a closed room.

Soul calls for you to set your spirit free to nourish all that matters in your life.

Yellow/White   Earth/Heaven
Peace

We create our personal Heaven on Earth when Divine Will and personal Will act in harmony with the nature of the time.

These Runes call you to maintain balance and peace in your life.

Each person would define their Heaven on Earth differently. Some would emphasise love, others enlightenment, recreation, wisdom, or finding fulfilment through their occupation.

We construct our Heaven on Earth through the choices we make. Earth provides the things that we desire and Heaven provides the will to go and get them. On your true path your choices, boundaries and actions work in harmony with the nature of the time. In this way you cultivate your life and harvest your potential.

Desire cuts a path to what we want, but Heaven's Will and personal Will converge along the middle path. The middle way of action maintains balance in our lives, working in accordance with the nature of our time.

To meet others midway it is necessary to be moderate, willing to compromise and make sacrifices, without forcing one's opinion or presence on them, and not making them feel inferior, for acts of this sort are divisive. They foster envy and create factions.

To maintain peace in your life it is necessary to be tolerant and understanding with those who rock your boat, not being drawn aside by their overbearing influence, manipulation or flattery, and not assuming that you are superior in any way.

Yellow/Blue   Earth/Water
Recovery through Leadership

In a fertile and abundant landscape there is just enough

groundwater. Sometimes in some places groundwater must be channelled to benefit the crops.

These Runes call you to fight for what is right, to take the lead and recover what is lost.

A bond is broken: in oneself this may be through loss of personal integrity; a dishonourable act or breaking one's word.

In relationship to others it may be through one person taking too much for themselves; leaving others feeling depleted, drained, threatened or undernourished.

The Water element in our lives guides us to follow the main road, the path of least resistance.

The natural flow is disrupted when people leave the main road for the sidetrack, seeking pleasure in the wrong things. For recovery the heart and mind must be congruent and one must have the courage to surrender what is not rightfully theirs.

This calls for a down to earth approach, to touch base with oneself and with those that one would lead, understanding the nourishment that one another need.

When one has gained too much or taken what is not rightfully theirs, security becomes an issue and fear of loss motivates the need to defend what has been gained.

To successfully retrieve what has been taken away there must be mutual respect between the leader and those who are led. The cause must be valid and just, the aims clear and the task well organised. The use of force must be the last resort.

Yellow/Purple   Earth/Mountain
Modesty

Mountain gives way to valley so that all may be nourished.

These Runes call you to know the balance that modesty maintains, for when something is too full it spills over, and when too empty it is filled.

Water like modesty is enduring, without striving it wears down mountains and fills up valleys. We shape our lives through the way we behave.

Modesty requires restraint and self-discipline to maintain balance between giving and taking, and to do this without putting on airs. False claims have to be made to gain what is not rightfully ours, and then others lose what should be theirs. Through modesty, one surrenders to one's destiny.

It is unwise to glory in one's achievements and position for it is a law of nature to empty what is full and to fill what is empty.

The wise are modest, therefore they pose no threat and they do not have to struggle or fight to hold on to what is rightfully theirs.

The modest way is not passive but influential, it does not deny one's value, but being inoffensive meets no resistance. In dealing with others it is gentle and kind, speaking only the truth and acting justly.

Yellow/Green   Earth/Thunder
Returning after Separation

Thunder sleeps within the Earth – untapped potential for transformation. Thunder must awaken before it can burst forth to bring new life.

These Runes greet you at a crossroads in your life, alerting you that you have been sidetracked for long enough. Pause now to review where you are, consider how you got to this point in your life, and how you will return to the path of wholeness.

On the journey towards wholeness you choose your own directions and the turns to take; sometimes failing to see the bigger picture you make poor choices, and become attached to certain parts of your life, neglecting the rest. As you deviate further from wholeness your wounds don't heal. Finally exhaustion or crisis stop you in your tracks, shake you up, and cause you to reassess where you are and realise the errors of your ways.

Consider how you have become separated from your true path. Review your life story so far, and the circumstances and choices that led to where you are now.

Contemplate how you feel about your life right now, and what changes you must make to feel more whole. The call for action is further along your path.

You must prepare yourself for this time, take time out for recreation, to treat yourself tenderly and with care. Nourish your roots and strengthen yourself through rest, recuperation and understanding.

You are the author of your own life story so pay attention to who and what you include in your script.

Some people, places and things are destined to play a part in your life: you will find them on the main road towards wholeness.

Yellow/Orange   Earth/Wind
Just Do what Must be Done

With your feet firmly on the ground, walking your path with devotion, flexibility and the Will to endure, you will not be blown astray.

These Runes call you to get on with your life, being present in each moment, following your calling with the Will to do what must be done, so that your Will and Divine Will work together.

Life is a pilgrimage. We walk through the valleys of our shadows revisiting the aspects of ourselves that we find most difficult. It is a journey home, and at the end of the journey, having covered no distance at all, we come to know our place as if for the first time and we are transformed. Along the way we shed tears of joy and pain that fall like rain to wash our feet and clean the path for others to follow in our steps.

The ego struggles with mortality. In a world of illusions it is hard to let go of life's attachments. When you walk your true path centred in your own being nothing can really wound you.

Know that you are an explorer on this journey through life, so don't push forward through blind impulse, always be mindful and conscientious, not skipping any stages of your development. The ego wants to reach its goal quickly and skip the parts of life that are difficult.

You must follow your deeper calling, walking every step of the way, just doing what must be done with modesty and flexibility.

Nourish your roots so they will grow strong, so you may yield to external influences like a tree swaying in the wind. One needs endurance, devotion and constancy to follow one's true path.

Be mindful of the people who share your path, for these enter your circle of belonging. Be open, kind and nourishing towards them, but remember you are the pioneer in your own life story.

Maintain your personal honour and integrity and don't get sidetracked by others. As you grow, others grow with you.

Yellow/ Red   *Earth/Fire*
The Dark Night

Fire in the depths of the Earth when all around is darkness and you must make your way amongst your shadows until the light of day returns.

These Runes call you to experience inner growth at difficult times when your outer experiences cannot be changed.

You are in the midst of, or about to enter, difficult times. This must be so, for the light that follows darkness shines much brighter than before. Life seems to plot against you, it tests you to the limit, and you are wounded. When victims point at others they give their power away, for no one else can be responsible for the way a person feels. Those who inflict the wounds are messengers, they bring your demons home for you to fight them in the darkness of yourself. Don't focus on the messenger.

This is a trial by fire, a test of your resolve. When the pain is great, will you renounce what you believe in? You may need to swallow your pride, but not your honour and dignity. Don't give yourself away.

Enter the wound to heal it, there is no point in breaking free from what necessity brings; you are bound to journey inwards, to confront the demons in your shadows – yield and you will overcome.

Shine a light unto yourself, this will heal your wounds and brighten the armour of your spirit.

This is not a time for external achievement, but a time for

caution and reserve. In dealing with others: shine, but not to blind them. Tell the truth but don't drag them into your light. Don't be hasty or aggressive in settling disputes. Don't harbour expectations and judgements. For the moment let them be.

Turquoise/Clear   *Lake/Unity*
No Regrets

> Do not grieve for what you cannot have.
> Do not grieve for what you cannot know.
> Do not grieve for life that has now past:
> Anoint your dead and let them go.
> Make your peace with what was never said,
> and with all that never was to be.
> Never want to have your time again,
> just say and do what must be said and done.
> Let the heart rest in peace.
> No regrets – Life is your present.

Turquoise/Turquoise   *Lake/Lake*
True Joy

Joy brings comfort to our lives. We look at people, projects and things to see whether they will bring us joy, and when we are attracted to them we welcome them into our circle of belonging. But how do we find them, how do we choose who and what to let in?

We find true joy when our choices rest on the truth and strength within us. Lacking this guidance we look for pleasure at the surface, swept along by the attractions, temptations and pleasures that are the ego's choice.

Ask yourself, what will you exchange for joy? To find true joy you must be prepared to make sacrifices, to give up certain attachments that block your joy from flowing freely. True joy outpours from love and truth, it is a font of well-being, always there, not compromised by tit-for-tat relationships or this for that exchanges. Joy is not a gift that comes attached to something else: it rises from within you.

The release of pain brings pleasure, but this is not true joy, because it is attached to woundedness and neediness. Relationships are often bound together by insecurity, not love, people sticking together because "he (or she) needs me", or "without this relationship where would I be"?

Be with those who help you find joy in who you truly are, for destiny calls you to "Know yourself". This is not solely an inward journey, nor is it lonely, it takes you outside yourself, to share your joy in good company.

The joy of knowing oneself is the greatest gift one can give to the world. How you know yourself is the foundation for everything you do. Lack of this knowing causes the deepest wounds of our time, affecting not only our personal lives but all our relationships and connections. Knowing yourself you will know that you are beautiful and good, though often your behaviour may not follow.

Bless the world in your knowing, reach out in an open and friendly way, so that others will find joy in your heart.

The words "If only" put your life on hold. Don't wait for another day or another opportunity, find the place where joy is blocked and make some changes to let it flow.

Turquoise/White   Lake/Heaven
To be Creative

A heavenly lake of creative abundance, bearing gifts for oneself and the world.

These Runes call you to cultivate the grounds for your creativity, and share your beauty with the world.

Life is an act of creation; everything we think, say and do, through every moment of our lives, is creative.

Creativity is all about us: in the present moment, in the influences of the past and the calling of the future.

Heaven calls us to be effective, to make choices that lead towards the ultimate goal of life's experience – to fulfil our destiny.

In Lake we find joy in the seeds that Heaven sows, we penetrate its depths to realise what must be done, and the world profits from the fruits of our creativity.

To be "yourself" is your greatest design, and to love yourself is the only way to achieve this. This is your greatest service to the world, for we create the world through the way we see ourselves.

In cultivating who you really are, you must weed out all that is inappropriate. This calls for a thorough self-examination, leaving no stone unturned. But do not enter into a battle with yourself or others. Meeting force with force is not the creative way to achieve good. Nourish the root to enjoy the fruit.

Dwelling on problems, and longing for qualities one does not yet possess, fuel inner conflict. Simply be ready to meet change when it comes, and be at home with the qualities you already have. Forcing changes and being obstinate about getting what you want blocks the creative flow. You must be cautious about timing, wakeful to what's happening and well-considered in taking action. Misguided creativity draws one to lose sight of who they are and to forget their calling.

Cultivate your potential as a gift you have to share.

Turquoise/Blue   *Lake/Water*
Entering the Wound

A Lake that does not hold Water: little nourishment enters the well-spring of your life, and fate deals a heavy blow that is necessary for your personal development.

These Runes call you to realise that these difficult times are a training-ground for your later success. Nothing expansive can be achieved at this time, for now it is necessary to journey inward, to realise the nature of your condition and change your way of thinking so your experience will reflect the way you truly are.

As you find the way to truly nourish your life, the waters again will rise through the depths of the Lake. To achieve this you must realise your self-worth and follow your true path in life. This requires letting go of negative beliefs that do not serve you, cleansing your life and making sacrifices.

Find the inner strength to bend with adversity and learn from your experience. You may consider this time to be a baptism – an initiation experience; then the way you handle this trial of life will determine what happens in the next generation of your experience.

Happiness, health and abundance are conditions that arise from the natural flow of life-force energy (*Ki*). Energy follows thought and our thoughts take shape in our lives. So thinking that does not serve the truth of who you are will manifest as a problem - a wound that you must enter in order to experience the truth.

There is always a lighter side to any problem, so try to see the humour in your situation - for often life, it seems, is a tragic comedy, and cheerfulness is a good road to recovery.

Turquoise/Purple   Lake/Mountain
Influence through Humility

The Mountain peak gives way to the Lake as humility replaces pride. The open and receptive are welcomed to this high position. Lake in this position becomes a reservoir of clean and pure water, to serve and prosper all who stand below it.

These Runes call you to consider your influence. How pure are your intentions, and how open and receptive to influence are you?

Humility has strength. Through humility you can live with criticism because you truly love yourself, and others are attracted to this quiet power. So know how to stand firm, to feel good about yourself, and forgive the transgressions of others. Don't give yourself away by yielding to every whim of those you choose to serve, for that would be humiliating.

It would be humiliating to vent your anger on someone else, but anger stored must be released, so you must find a positive outlet, for anger bottled up eats away at life. Until there is forgiveness it is hard to let go of anger.

Humility is built upon honesty and compassion. Manipulation and striving to influence invites humiliation. Nothing enduring will come from manipulating the truth. To court positivity one must try to see the good in every situation, and something of beauty in the words and deeds of all people.

Turquoise/Green   Lake/Thunder
Following

Thunder awakes in the depths of the Lake. Bathed in innocence authority arises.

These Runes call you to pay attention to how you develop your authority and the example you set for others to follow. They also prompt you to consider your motivation for who and what you choose to follow.

He who knows himself and loves himself is the best authority. This one follows his true path and others follow him joyfully, knowing that dignity and honour will be present on the journey. So become this one.

When you are playing roles, people cannot know you for who you truly are. Other people need your good influence, but you must find the way.

Sometimes it is necessary to rest and bide the time before movement. Forcing or manipulating a situation runs contrary to the nature of the time. One needs to learn how to adapt to the times and to respect the needs of others.

How can people follow when you are in their face? Get out of their way – stand behind them, give them space, encouragement, and inspiration, for you are not their saviour but a simple messenger.

Remind yourself of this when someone tries to become attached to you, for you are simply the place through which your genius enters the world.

By the light of who you are others may be guided to know their own genius, so pay attention to what you think.

Your thinking should follow the higher path so that genius can find its way into your behaviour. Through this ascent you open the way for others to follow.

Turquoise/Orange   *Lake/Wind*
Great Changes

An invisible wind blows beneath the Lake, stirring the under-currents of your life to penetrate the depths of your identity and to bring great changes in the way you live your life.

These Runes call you to be in the flow of these changing times, to recognize that these Winds of change blow from your inside outward, and that you cannot resist their flow. You must decide how to move with them, and where you are coming from.

The physical world is always a reflection of the invisible world. As your inner world changes, you break away from external situations that cannot change with you, and from attachments that do not serve your higher purpose.

Don't look to others for your strength because you will not find it there, and don't look for security on another person's path, because this will lead you in the wrong direction. They will sense that you are changing and their fears may undermine your resolve. You must be firm but gentle in dealing with the outside world.

There will be major obstacles to overcome and you must find the strength to do this for yourself. Nothing can be achieved by force and striving, only through gentle perseverance and commitment to your path.

The Divine calls you to recognise the vows of your sacred marriage to love and honour yourself, and to find your own way in the outside world.

Turquoise/Red   *Lake/Fire*
Handling Discontent

Fire trapped in the darkness of Lake, the heart is explosive with desire for change. How will you handle its release?

These Runes call you to consider how to handle discontent when an outmoded situation must change. You are called to consider where it is best to position yourself in this matter and where it is best to direct your attention.

Sometimes drastic measures are necessary to change a situation that is no longer appropriate, giving up something that is outmoded, like the shedding of a skin.

You may feel the need to break free, to come forward and stand out. Recognize the importance of good timing, do only what is possible to make the situation stable in the first instance.

If the desire for change is crushed, the energy to break free may implode, then changes will be subversive. With provocation the energy is explosive. Both ways are out of your control.

Lake influences the situation to show there is joy in following the right path. Being correct in one's authority is necessary, for people will only support what they feel to be just, and when the changes made are in their best interests without hidden agendas for personal gain.

To place oneself or others upon a pedestal is not in anyone's best interest. Respect for this position is only temporary; the exalted will be toppled and changes will be made. To covet or flaunt one's possessions or position draws attention for the wrong reasons, feeding the fires of desire that burn in others' hearts. Discontent and envy make hearts burn.

The Joy of Lake enlightens the situation. The warmth of Fire brings peace and contentment to the burning heart.

Turquoise/Yellow   *Lake/Earth*
Innocent Attraction

Earth in the place of Lake – all can see their own reflection in the surface of the Lake. The Lake nourishes all without discrimination.

These Runes call you to know that through being yourself, you illuminate and nourish the lives of others.

People need a firm centre around which to gather, they see in you what they need to cultivate in themselves. Through courage you make your place in the world, a subtle place of influence that creates small ripples of change in other people's lives.

People who belong together must come together, they must

yield to their attraction, for they understand each other.

The world is a reflection of the way people are themselves. If you can be true to yourself, doing only what you believe in, with a joyful attitude and to the best of your ability, other people will see your self-esteem and be impressed with your self-discipline. In this way you become a beacon to others, and you can have a great effect upon the world.

Retain your balance at the center through simplicity and innocence. Some will want to supplant you, others will want your company. Don't let their attention go to your head, for you don't need anyone's approval to be who you are. You must not be attached to their affections, for your position is based upon the way you love and honour yourself.

White/Clear   *Heaven/Unity*
Be Here Now

Enter the realm of Heaven to see beyond seeing, to feel beyond touch, to sense the invisible that calls you home to the here and now, to live your life as an everyday prayer.

Welcome to a time of reckoning: for you are the gatekeeper holding the keys to enlightenment. Just knock and the door will open, seek and you will find.

For just one moment put everything aside and take your place at the centre of your life to find silence and calm and make peace with your world. When you cannot see beyond suffering, worry, fear and regret, you have drawn a shroud across your life.

It is time to pierce the veil, to take a brighter view, for the gatekeeper has become the jailer and you are entrapped within your story. Right here, right now, you may break free to journey beyond your pleasure and pain to experience your life as an everyday prayer. From your center you can see the whole picture – it's just a story – see it, then reach beyond it, beyond the suffering of who you are in your story you will find enlightenment in who you truly are.

Attune your senses, for you may see, hear, taste, touch and smell without limitation, for your senses are portals into the hidden depths of your sensational life.

Be here now, and then again and again, extending this moment until you can see that it could last forever; for no matter what is happening in your story, every moment is an everyday prayer.

White/White   *Heaven/Heaven*
Life's Calling

You are meant to be here, and to find your place in the world, for your presence makes a difference.

Guidance comes to you from the primal depths of the universe, calling you to do what must be done. Your Divine path helps you to realise your potential to manifest your true qualities in the world, and to take your place in the great harmony of existence.

Consider your Life's Calling:

Are you living a life that is truly yours?

Do you feel you are fulfilling your destiny?

Do you walk your path with compassion for others?

Can you see how other people benefit from your existence?

Each person has their own unique purpose in life; not necessarily a job description, or a goal to be reached before life's end, but a path, a way of being in the world that touches the lives of others, and fulfills one's own true nature.

Along the way, life greets you with opportunities to progress your divinely chosen path, calling you to pay attention to the qualities of your home, your health, and your relationships. Look at them, they bring to light the shadow side of your nature and present your wounds for healing. They help you to question who you truly are and what you are meant to do.

As you find your place in the world, the world moves with you closer towards peace.

White/Blue   Heaven/Water
Resolving Conflict

Heaven is control and Water is flow. You have come to a crossroads where your way is hindered by an obstacle or an opposition. Your Will and Divine Will are in conflict.

These Runes call you to consider your motives before making your next move. When there is clarity at the outset and rights and responsibilities are clearly defined, then unnecessary conflict can be avoided. But now the conflict has begun there is something to be learned from the way it is resolved.

External conflict is a reflection of inner conflict. This situation may be necessary for you to make a breakthrough or a discovery, or it may be halting you, providing a chance to reconsider the way you are going.

Going with the flow sometimes calls for yielding, retreating or giving way; and sometimes it requires reinforcing boundaries, pushing forward or standing your ground. To choose what is appropriate at this time you must first question your motives:

What inner conflict does this stem from?

What is truly at stake here and how much does it really matter?

Are you being honest in the way you are dealing with this situation?

Are you following your truth or is your ego leading through pride, vanity, or the need for conquest?

Have you considered the opposite points of view?

There is no need to fear the consequences of doing what you truly believe in; often it is brave to retreat or at least to meet the opposition half way.

White/Purple   Heaven/Mountain
Keeping your own Counsel

Heaven on the Mountain calls for clear sight and tactful reserve.

These Runes call you to be awake, courteous, yielding, simple and receptive. Other people move in and out of your life story and you move in and out of theirs. In your relationship with them there are times to exert your influence and times to hold yourself in dignified reserve.

Your own attitude of mind extends into your relationships. A peaceful mind knows the time to speak with courteous words that are penetrating yet compassionate; at other times it keeps its own counsel, remaining watchful, seeing the simplicity in all things, and being open and receptive to alternative points of view.

The inner conflict of a troubled mind extends into relationships. Sometimes the ego and the Will want to exert their influence in inappropriate ways.

Heaven helps you to see through situations whilst remaining detached from the need to have an influence. Mountain helps you to maintain a good perspective, knowing that people will come to you when their time is right. So pause, contemplate, center yourself and adjust to the situation, taking action only when the time is right.

You bind yourself to trouble when you become attached to a judgement or embroiled in a situation where you have over-extended your influence. This takes your energy; it is better to hold your energy in dignified reserve.

These elements play themselves out through many social inter-actions. Often we must work with their presence silently through a positive attitude of mind, but sometimes it is necessary physically to withdraw, to find sanctuary and regain strength and composure.

White/Green　　　　　*Heaven/Thunder*
Return to Innocence

On the spiritual journey we are eternally children, forever at the beginning.

Heaven and Thunder wake us up to the world and make an orphan of our innocence. Then they guide our return so we may discover that freedom means little until it is lost.

These Runes call us to know that Heaven's Will and Blessings go with us when we return to Innocence. Progress through wilfulness or trying to control outcomes, is in opposition to one's fate.

Original Innocence cannot be clothed, groomed or educated, it is a natural state of freedom; wisdom without knowledge, freedom without boundaries, unsullied by earthly influence.

Innocence is never lost, only submerged beneath the masks we wear. The return to Innocence heals the wounds of the eternal child, the blows to the spirit that accompany us throughout our lives.

It heals through understanding and forgiveness, knowing that to understand, one must stand under and let truth rain down from above.

Innocence adopts this position, for it comes to understanding with willingness to welcome the unexpected and accept the unexplainable. It breaks free from the walled enclosure and chooses the winding road, for it knows there is freedom in an open mind, and magic in changing directions.

It is comfortable with paradox, for this is the way of the Divine. Problems are, in fact, opportunities on the road to recovery, engaging one during the journeying process.

Innocence is different from naivety and has little in common with ignorance. Innocence is a sanctuary free from injury and pain. It avoids harming, and when harm is done it is willing to repair.

In sleep we all return to Innocence: our body, mind and soul unite to heal the scars of the day. Then to what do we awake, how long does it take for the adult mind to pull itself together and forget where it has been.

How wonderful it can be to go through the day in a state of alert Innocence, knowing that what you seek also seeks you, being still for just long enough to enjoy the destiny in every moment.

White/Orange   Heaven/Wind
Gently Controlling

These Runes call you to take responsibility for your life. You cannot outrun this Heavenly Wind, nor can you hide. You must decide how to meet it, assuming your best posture in relation to the mechanisms of change that penetrate your life right now.

In this situation you are losing authority over your life. People, situations and ideas can help to guide your way, but at this time they may be assuming too much influence in your life. Temptations, ambitions, false promises and flattery are all mechanisms by which you can lose your way. Now you must consider your position:

Are you on the path of your highest potential?

Do the influences in your life truly support you?

Are you exercising enough control?

The path that leads you here calls you to establish your own boundaries and limitations for behaviour.

Be patient and tolerant in meeting others half way, but go no further. Do not give yourself away by sacrificing your honour and dignity to other people, situations or ideas.

Be strong, true and unswerving, but do not act without due care and attention. Find the way to be gentle yet penetrating, not hard and reactive.

White/Red   Heaven/Fire
Clear and Binding Agreements

Clarity and Truth shine in Heaven and people commit to act honourably and fairly. Your word is your bond.

These Runes call you to see your promises and agreements as sacred contracts. To give one's word may be morally and legally binding, but more than this, it binds one's spirit to a condition of service.

When entering into an agreement, be clear about your position and your expectations. You will need to be flexible, not controlling, if you are to achieve something that is of mutual benefit.

First contemplate the conditions of your agreement to understand the truth. Be careful not to deceive yourself, and don't be fooled by appearances. Through being modest and acting with humility you may be underestimated – this gives you an advantage that is not unfair, provided your dealings have been open and honest. Just take care not to underestimate others.

If one is honest and fair there is no need to hide when people say things that are not true about you, for their gossip has no foundation. The dishonest, deceitful and manipulative become prisoners of their own intentions.

The words you exchange with others create conditions, so be aware of what you say, for your energy, spirit and providence follow your intentions.

White/Yellow   Heaven/Earth
Attunement and Co-ordination

Heaven and Earth are out of communion.

These Runes call you at a time when certain parts of your life are breaking apart or breaking down, and you feel torn. There is no quick fix and nothing to be gained by continuing this way or by maintaining this status quo.

Action is called for, but first you must bide your time to establish inner calm. Fate will show the way. Just be open, patient and persevering, then co-ordinate your whole being to work in harmony with the time, to do what must be done.

Inner and outer voices influence your life, pulling you this way and that, rocking your boat until you do not know the way to go.

Soul calls to you to follow your true path. Your ego and some of the people in your life ask you to make some bad decisions and you are torn between your affections, your duties and associations. The voice of Victim, Servant, and Martyr, coax you the wrong way saying: *"I have no choice, it is my duty, and they need me".*

Attune yourself to your higher calling, for you reign sovereign over the landscape of your life. You have been ordained into this life to do what must be done.

Your Sacred calling is personal to you, it does not call you to please the others or follow their path, it calls for you to go your own way and to be your own life coach.

Soul knows the people and the places where you belong, and will guide you to the company of good companions and good advice. You may suffer loss along the way, so be it. Stand your ground – be brave – stand up for what you believe in and withdraw from what is wrong. Expect to encounter internal and external conflict by going this way, for you rock the status quo in the circle of family, friends and acquaintances.

The empowered voice of Victim, Servant and Martyr calls you to break free from your physical and mental bondage saying: *"Follow the enlightened path to be victorious, to serve your higher nature, and surrender to the heartfelt calling of your Soul".*

White/Turquoise   Heaven/Lake
Helpful Friends

The horizon between Heaven and Lake: these Runes call you to perceive the horizon where all our viewpoints meet. It is a great leveller from which we draw a true perspective.

Even friends find it hard to be authentic, playing roles that fit their story and casting judgements to satisfy their script.

We like to know where we are coming from. We like to see things in a certain way. When people and circumstances cannot be placed within the context of our stories we feel insecure. When things don't fit, it is easier to write them off, saying they are not relevant or not worthy of attention. To understand another person you must first step outside your story, because understanding is a humble pursuit in which one is fully present and open to receive the truth.

When you feel you have an enlightened point of view, that you can see the way for others and you want to go to their aid, question your intentions. What motivates you to help them? Do you have ulterior motives? Are you trying too hard or forcing your Will upon them without respecting their boundaries? Each person requires a certain touch. To be welcome you must first be sensitive to their needs. You have no right to enter uninvited through the layers of protection that shield their vulnerabilities, only they can open the way for you.

Often people will play the Good Samaritan and the Martyr, when really they need help themselves. They give so much and get little in return. If you assume an elevated position then others may fail to see that you are vulnerable as well. Elevation is not enlightenment; it accompanies pride, arrogance, dominance and boasting. Elevation creates separation and causes feelings to be hurt.

Sometimes you may sense a call for help, but the way to enter seems blocked. First let down your guard so they may let down theirs. They will open to you when you step outside the role you are playing.

Shed the illusions that come between you and other people and gain a more enlightened view through being aware of your intimate connections with them.

When you are authentic you let down your guard and breathe life in, you make life welcome in you. To understand anything one must first breathe it in, to be with it.

Help and Support to Cope with Change.

Most commonly people work with homesouls because they want something to change in their life. Often changes do not come in the way we expect them, and sometimes in the process of change there are uncomfortable issues that we have to deal with along the way.

I have given lots of examples in the book of how changes sometimes occur. In the two most detailed stories, both Esther and Diana are experienced therapists, both are well placed to deal with changes in their lives, and both have plenty of support through other therapists and friends who understand what they are going through. In their story, big changes took place, and this happened over a long period of time.

Often when doing this work, changes happen more quickly, and sometimes they catch us unprepared to deal with the fall out. So I want to make this recommendation, please make sure you have some support when you go into this work. We all need someone to talk to who can help us to take a wider view and to see things from a distance, so we don't get too tied up in the story.

I have found the way to get the most out of this work is to do it with a group of friends meeting regularly to track the changes in their lives; to be there if support is needed, and to lighten up the journey.

Login at www.homesouls.com if you want some tips on setting up a group, or taking part in a group, or if you simply want to find out more and have some contact with others who are doing this work.

To purchase the Glass Runes or the homesouls Oracle Cards go to www.glassrunes.com or www.homesouls.com

Suggested further reading

- *Imagery in Healing, Shamanism and Modern Medicine* Jeanne Achterberg (Shambhala , 2002)
- *Imagination is Reality* Roberts Avens (Spring publications, 2003)
- *The Poetics of Space* Gaston Bachelard (Beacon Press, 1972)
- *Finding Your Own North Star* Martha Beck (Piatkus, 2001)
- *The Book of Runes* Ralph Blum (Headline, 1995)
- *The Relationship Runes* Ralph Blum (Connections)
- *The Healing Runes* Ralph Blum (Connections)
- *The Artist's Way* Julia Cameron (Pan, 1995)
- *The Druid Renaissance* Philip Carr-Gomm (Thorsons, 1996)
- *Lewis Carroll, The Complete Fully Illustrated Works* Lewis Carroll (Gramercy)
- *House as a Mirror of Self ~ Exploring the Deeper Meaning of Home* Clare Cooper Marcus (Conari Press, 1997)
- *The Meaning of Things ~ Domestic Symbols and the Self* Mihaly Csikszentmihalyi and Eugene Rochberg-Halton (Cambridge University Press, 1999)
- *Places of the Soul* Christopher Day (Aquarian Press, 1990)
- *Tao Te Ching* Gia-Fu Feng and Jane English (Wildwood House, 1982)
- *Re-Visioning Psychology* James Hillman (Harper Perennial, 1992)
- *The Tao of Pooh* Benjamin Hoff (Mandarin, 1989)
- *Man and his Symbols* Carl Jung (Picador, 1978)
- *Synchronicity ~ an Acausal Connecting Principle* Carl Jung (Ark, 1995)
- *Creating Sacred Space with Feng Shui* Karen Kingston (Piatkus, 1996)
- *Ladies of the Lake* Caitlin and John Mathews (The Aquarian Press, 1992)
- *Sacred Contracts* Caroline Myss (Harmony Books, 2001)
- *Eternal Echoes ~ Exploring our Hunger to Belong* John O'Donohue (Bantam, 1998)
- *Divine Beauty ~ the Invisible Embrace* John O'Donohue (Bantam Press)

- *Women Who Run with the Wolves* Clarissa Pinkola Estes (Rider, 1998)
- *The Gentle Art of Blessing* Pierre Pradervand (Cygnus, 2003)
- *The Complete Guide to Nine Star Ki* Bob Sachs (Element, 1992)
- *What the Bee Knows* P L Travers (Arkana, 1993)
- *I Ching ~ Book of Changes* Richard Wilhelm translation (Arkana, 1989)
- *The Celtic Wheel of Life* Andy Baggott (Gateway Books)

BOOKS

O books

O is a symbol of the world, of oneness and unity. In different cultures it also means the "eye", symbolizing knowledge and insight, and in Old English it means "place of love or home". O books explores the many paths of understanding which different traditions have developed down the ages, particularly those today that express respect for the planet and all of life.

For more information on the full list of over 300 titles please visit our website
www.O-books.net

Back to the Truth
5,000 years of Advaita
Dennis Waite

A wonderful book. Encyclopedic in nature, and destined to become a classic. **James Braha**
  Absolutely brilliant…an ease of writing with a water-tight argument outlining the great universal truths. This book will become a modern classic. A milestone in the history of Advaita. **Paula Marvelly**

1905047614 500pp **£19.95 $29.95**

Beyond Photography
Encounters with orbs, angels and mysterious light forms
Katie Hall and John Pickering

The authors invite you to join them on a fascinating quest; a voyage of discovery into the nature of a phenomenon, manifestations of which are shown as being historical and global as well as contemporary and intently personal.
  At journey's end you may find yourself a believer, a doubter or simply an intrigued wonderer… Whatever the outcome, the process of journeying is likely prove provocative and stimulating and - as with the mysterious images fleetingly captured by the authors' cameras - inspiring and potentially enlightening. **Brian Sibley**, author and broadcaster.

1905047908 272pp 50 b/w photos +8pp colour insert **£12.99 $24.95**

Don't Get MAD Get Wise
Why no one ever makes you angry, ever!
Mike George

There is a journey we all need to make, from anger, to peace, to forgiveness. Anger always destroys, peace always restores, and forgiveness always heals. This explains the journey, the steps you can take to make it happen for you.

1905047827 160pp **£7.99 $14.95**

IF You Fall...
It's a new beginning
Karen Darke

Karen Darke's story is about the indomitability of spirit, from one of life's cruel vagaries of fortune to what is insight and inspiration. She has overcome the limitations of paralysis and discovered a life of challenge and adventure that many of us only dream about. It is all about the mind, the spirit and the desire that some of us find, but which all of us possess.
Joe Simpson, mountaineer and author of *Touching the Void*

1905047886 240pp **£9.99 $19.95**

Love, Healing and Happiness
Spiritual wisdom for a post-secular era
Larry Culliford

This will become a classic book on spirituality. It is immensely practical and grounded. It mirrors the author's compassion and lays the foundation for a higher understanding of human suffering and hope.
Reinhard Kowalski, Consultant Clinical Psychologist

1905047916 304pp **£10.99 $19.95**

A Map to God
Awakening Spiritual Integrity
Susie Anthony

This describes an ancient hermetic pathway, representing a golden thread running through many traditions, which offers all we need to understand and do to actually become our best selves.

1846940443 260pp **£10.99 $21.95**

Punk Science
Inside the mind of God
Manjir Samanta-Laughton

Wow! Punk Science is an extraordinary journey from the microcosm of the atom to the macrocosm of the Universe and all stops in between. Manjir Samanta-Laughton's synthesis of cosmology and consciousness is sheer genius. It is elegant, simple and, as an added bonus, makes great reading. **Dr Bruce H. Lipton**, author of *The Biology of Belief*

1905047932 320pp **£12.95 $22.95**

Rosslyn Revealed
A secret library in stone
Alan Butler

Rosslyn Revealed gets to the bottom of the mystery of the chapel featured in the Da Vinci Code. The results of a lifetime of careful research and study demonstrate that truth really is stranger than fiction; a library of philosophical ideas and mystery rites, that were heresy in their time, have been disguised in the extraordinarily elaborate stone carvings.

1905047924 260pp b/w + colour illustrations **£19.95 $29.95** cl

The Way of Thomas
Nine Insights for Enlightened Living from the Secret Sayings of Jesus
John R. Mabry

What is the real story of early Christianity? Can we find a Jesus that is relevant as a spiritual guide for people today?

These and many other questions are addressed in this popular presentation of the teachings of this mystical Christian text. Includes a reader-friendly version of the gospel.

1846940303 196pp **£10.99 $19.95**

The Way Things Are
A Living Approach to Buddhism
Lama Ole Nydahl

An up-to-date and revised edition of a seminal work in the Diamond Way Buddhist tradition (three times the original length), that makes the timeless wisdom of Buddhism accessible to western audiences. Lama Ole has established more than 450 centres in 43 countries.

1846940427 240pp **£9.99 $19.95**

The 7 Ahas! of Highly Enlightened Souls
How to free yourself from ALL forms of stress
Mike George

7th printing
A very profound, self empowering book. Each page bursting with wisdom and insight. One you will need to read and reread over and over again! Paradigm Shift. I totally love this book, a wonderful nugget of inspiration. **PlanetStarz**

1903816319 128pp 190/135mm **£5.99 $11.95**

God Calling
A Devotional Diary
A. J. Russell

46th printing
"When supply seems to have failed, you must know that it has not
done so. But you must look around to see what you can give away.
Give away something." One of the best-selling devotional books of
all time, with over 6 million copies sold.

1905047428 280pp 135/95mm **£7.99** cl.
US rights sold

The Goddess, the Grail and the Lodge
The Da Vinci code and the real origins of religion
Alan Butler

5th printing
*This book rings through with the integrity of sharing time-honoured
revelations. As a historical detective, following a golden thread from the
great Megalithic cultures, Alan Butler vividly presents a compelling
picture of the fight for life of a great secret and one that we simply can't
afford to ignore.* **Lynn Picknett & Clive Prince**

1903816696 360pp 230/152mm **£12.99 $19.95**

The Heart of Tantric Sex
A unique guide to love and sexual fulfilment
Diana Richardson

3rd printing
The art of keeping love fresh and new long after the honeymoon is
over. Tantra for modern Western lovers adapted in a practical,
refreshing and sympathetic way.

One of the most revolutionary books on sexuality ever written. **Ruth Ostrow**, News Ltd.
1903816378 256pp **£9.99 $14.95**

I Am With You
The best-selling modern inspirational classic
John Woolley

14th printing hardback
Will bring peace and consolation to all who read it. **Cardinal Cormac Murphy-O'Connor**

0853053413 280pp 150x100mm **£9.99** cl
4th printing paperback
1903816998 280pp 150/100mm **£6.99 $12.95**

In the Light of Meditation
The art and practice of meditation in 10 lessons
Mike George

2nd printing
A classy book. A gentle yet satisfying pace and is beautifully illustrated. Complete with a CD or guided meditation commentaries, this is a true gem among meditation guides. **Brainwave**
In-depth approach, accessible and clearly written, a convincing map of the overall territory and a practical path for the journey. **The Light**

1903816610 224pp 235/165mm full colour throughout +CD **£11.99 $19.95**

The Instant Astrologer
A revolutionary new book and software package for the astrological seeker
Lyn Birkbeck

2nd printing
The brilliant Lyn Birkbeck's new book and CD package, The Instant Astrologer, combines modern technology and the wisdom of the ancients, creating an invitation to enlightenment for the masses, just when we need it most!
Astrologer **Jenny Lynch**, Host of NYC's StarPower Astrology Television Show

1903816491 628pp full colour throughout with CD ROM 240/180 **£39 $69** cl

Is There An Afterlife?
A comprehensive overview of the evidence, from east and west
David Fontana

2nd printing
An extensive, authoritative and detailed survey of the best of the evidence supporting survival after death. It will surely become a classic not only of parapsychology literature in general but also of survival literature in particular. **Universalist**
1903816904 496pp 230/153mm **£14.99 $24.95**

The Reiki Sourcebook
Bronwen and Frans Stiene

5th printing
It captures everything a Reiki practitioner will ever need to know about the ancient art. This book is hailed by most Reiki professionals as the best guide to Reiki. For an average reader, it's also highly enjoyable and a good

way to learn to understand Buddhism, therapy and healing. **Michelle Bakar**, B*eauty magazine*
1903816556 384pp **£12.99 $19.95**

Soul Power
The transformation that happens when you know
Nikki de Carteret

4th printing
One of the finest books in its genre today. Using scenes from her own life and growth, Nikki de Carteret weaves wisdom about soul growth and the power of love and transcendent wisdom gleaned from the writings of the mystics. This is a book that I will read gain and again as a reference for my own soul growth. **Barnes and Noble review**

190381636X 240pp **£9.99 $15.95**

How to Meet Yourself
...and find true happiness
Dennis Waite

A comprehensive survey of the psychological and philosophical dynamics of the human condition, offering an everlasting solution to discovering true happiness in the moment. I highly recommend it. Dennis Waite is one of the foremost contemporary writers on Advaita Vedanta in the West. **Paula Marvelly**, author of *The Teachers of One*.

1846940419 260pp **£11.99 $24.95**